THE
BBC
PUZZLE BOOK

FRANCES
LINCOLN

First published in 2022
by Frances Lincoln,
an imprint of The Quarto Group.
The Old Brewery, 6 Blundell Street
London, N7 9BH,
United Kingdom
T (0)20 7700 6700
www.Quarto.com
© 2022 Quarto Publishing plc.

Text by Ian Smith
Puzzles by Dr Gareth Moore

By arrangement with the BBC.
The BBC logo is a trade mark of the British
Broadcasting Corporation and is used under license.

BBC logo © BBC 1996.

Every effort has been made to trace the copyright
holders of material quoted in this book.
If application is made in writing to the publisher,
any omissions will be included in future editions.

A catalogue record for this book is available
from the British Library.

ISBN 978-0-7112-7766-3

Ebook ISBN 978-0-7112-7767-0

10 9 8 7 6 5 4 3 2 1

Design by Dave Jones
Printed in China

THE
BBC
PUZZLE BOOK

Ian Smith
Dr Gareth Moore

FRANCES
LINCOLN

Contents

Introduction 6

    Timeline 8

    BBC Radio 12

    BBC TV 14

Entertainment 16

Drama 36

Comedy 70

Soap Opera 96

Sport 106

Music 114

Factual 126

Children's Television 154

Lifestyle 172

News, Weather and Current Affairs 184

Technology 206

Answers 214

Introduction

Developments in broadcasting at the end of the 19th century not only transformed communication between communities, cities and countries around the world, they made the planet a smaller place.

Guglielmo Marconi was pivotal in ushering in this revolution. In the early 1890s he began to develop an interest in 'wireless telegraphy', which was in its nascence. From there, he conducted experiments in radio waves, developing his own transmitter and receiver and, in 1895, he began transmitting signals over a short distance. An introduction to the Italian ambassador to London saw Marconi move to the United Kingdom and within a year he was demonstrating his equipment to the British government. On 13 May 1897, the first wireless communication was transmitted over open water, a 6-km (3¾-mile) distance between Flat Holm in the Bristol Channel to Lavernock Point, near Cardiff. Two months later, Marconi would found the Wireless Telegraph and Signal Company.

THE BBC IS BORN

It was from the factory floor of this business that the UK's first live public broadcast was made, featuring Australian soprano Dame Nellie Melba. A hit with audiences, it led to demands by various individuals and companies for licences to broadcast. Instead, the General Post Office, which oversaw the issuing of licences, decided to issue just one, to a consortium of companies whose joint name would be the British Broadcasting Company. At its head was John Reith. Over the next four years, it developed into the country's leading broadcaster. In 1927, Reith became the first Director-General of the British Broadcasting Corporation, whose Royal Charter saw it placed under the protection of the government and much of whose revenue is derived from its annual licence fee.

Strictly Come Dancing has garnered worldwide success for the BBC.

LEADING THE WORLD

This book is a journey through what happened next. Radio broadcasts were soon joined by television transmissions. As it grew in the 1930s, the BBC expanded its remit, offering a wider choice of news, entertainment and informative programming. The outbreak of the Second World War saw the organization become an integral part of the effort, both at home and around the world – the expansion of broadcasting in various countries continuing in peacetime with the World Service.

In the post-war years, the BBC expanded further, becoming the world's leading broadcaster. With each decade, the BBC embraced changes in both technology and society. Current affairs, comedy, drama and factual programming all evolved in tandem with shifting cultural and political tides. And as analogue became digital, and the Internet transformed the way we live and consume media, terrestrial broadcasting was surpassed by the unlimited avenues of online platforms.

This is a rich history, one that is described in detail in Professor David Hendy's comprehensive *The BBC: A People's History*. What this book sets out to do is offer highlights of the BBC's glorious past and to test your knowledge of it. From a world of soaps to scientific explorations, *Hancock's Half Hour* to *Fleabag*, *Doctor Who* to *I May Destroy You*, *The Archers* to *EastEnders*, each entry is accompanied by a variety of brain teasers to challenge, confound and celebrate 100 years of a national institution.

Radio

18 Oct. 1922
British Broadcasting Company forms

14 Nov. 1922
First radio broadcast from London

13 Feb. 1923
First broadcast from Wales

6 Mar. 1923
First broadcast from Scotland

28 Sept. 1923
Radio Times launches

15 Sept. 1924
First broadcast from N Ireland

1 Jan. 1927
The British Broadcasting
Company becomes the British
Broadcasting Corporation

15 Mar. 1932
The first radio broadcast is
made from Broadcasting House

19 Dec. 1932
The Empire Service
(precursor of the World Service)
launches on shortwave

1 Sept. 1939
Home Service begins

3 Sept. 1939
Chamberlain announces
start of WWII on the radio

3 Jan. 1938
The BBC's first foreign
language service, in
Arabic, begins airing

29 Jul. 1945
The Light
Programme begins

9 Oct. 1945
The first edition
of *Today in
Parliament* airs

29 Jan. 1942
*Desert Island
Discs* launches
and remains
on-air today

11 May 1940
A news service
broadcast in
Hindi begins

1920

1930

1940

Timeline

2 Nov. 1936
The BBC operates the
world's first regular
high-definition service,
from Alexandra Palace
in north London

2 June 1931
The first live television
outside broadcast takes
place from Epsom Derby

1 Sept. 1939
Television broadcasting
is suspended with the
outbreak of WWII

Television

29 Sept. 1946
The Third Programme begins

7 Oct. 1946
Woman's Hour offers
a dedicated radio show
for women

2 May 1955
The BBC begins
broadcasting its radio
service on FM

16 Jan. 1950
Listen with Mother launches
for the under-fives

1 Jan. 1951
The Archers
begins airing

28 Oct. 1957
The *Today* programme
begins broadcasting
on the Home Service

10 July 1969
Publication of the report 'Broadcasting
in the Seventies' results in a massive
overhaul of regional broadcasting

30 Sept. 1967
Radio 1 launches, plus
radio networks reorganize
into Radios 2, 3 and 4

18 Nov. 1967
The first local radio station
– BBC Radio Leicester –
begins broadcasting

4 Nov. 1972
Radios 2 and 4 begin
broadcasting in stereo

10 Sept. 1973
News bulletins
become a regular
feature of Radio 1

9 June 1975
Proceedings in
Parliament are
broadcast for
the first time

1950

1960

1970

5 Jan. 1948
The first news
programme
Newsreel
begins airing

20 Nov. 1947
An estimated 400,000
watch the wedding of
Princess Elizabeth to
Philip Mountbatten,
Duke of Edinburgh

7 June 1946
Television
broadcasting
resumes

25 Dec. 1957
The Queen's
Christmas Message
is broadcast for
the first time
on television

2 June 1953
The coronation of
Queen Elizabeth II is
watched live by an
estimated 20 million
people in the UK

20 Jul. 1969
22 million people
in the UK watch
the Moon Landing
on BBC TV

14 Sept. 1971
The *Nine O'Clock
News* begins airing
on BBC One

20 Apr. 1964
BBC Two starts
airing; existing
BBC TV channel is
renamed BBC One

20 June 1960
Nan Winton becomes the first
female national newsreader

23 Sept. 1974
The teletext
service Ceefax
begins operating

25 Sept. 1977
*The Morecambe & Wise
Christmas Show* attracts
a record audience of
over 28 million viewers

16 Jan. 1979
David Attenborough's
groundbreaking *Life On
Earth* begins airing

Radio

May 1989
BBC Night Network
launches on six local
radio stations, playing
throughout the night

25 Mar. 1990
BBC Radio 5
launches

Mar. 1998
The Radiophonic
Workshop closes its
doors after 40 years

31 Oct. 1987
Radio 1 starts
broadcasting on
FM in London

June 1996
Radio 1 starts
live-streaming
on the Internet

10 Sept. 1982
*Listen with
Mother* ends

27 Sept. 1995
Launch of
BBC national
radio on DAB

28 Mar. 1994
BBC Radio 5 Live
replaces BBC Radio 5

1980

1990

1 Dec. 1981
The BBC
Microcomputer
transforms
computer take-up

29 June 1981
The wedding of
Prince Charles
and Lady Diana
Spencer is watched
by an estimated
global audience
of 750 million

21 Nov. 1989
Television coverage
in the House of
Commons begins

13 Apr. 1994
The first BBC
website launches
on BBC Two's
computer show
The Net

29 Dec. 1996
The last episode of *Only
Fools and Horses* – before
the later one-off episodes
– attracts the largest
recorded sitcom audience
of 24.35 million viewers

17 Jan. 1983
Breakfast Time,
the UK's first
regular breakfast
TV service, begins

19 Feb. 1985
EastEnders launches
on BBC One

13 Jul. 1985
Live Aid, organized
by Bob Geldof,
transforms the globe

6 Sept. 1997
The funeral of Princess Diana
is broadcast to over 200
countries and a worldwide
audience of almost 3 billion

3 Sept. 1984
The Six O'Clock News is
broadcast on BBC One
for the first time

31 August 1991
BBC television begins officially
broadcasting in stereo
using the NICAM system

23 Sept. 1997
The BBC launches its first digital
TV channel BBC Choice, its first
television service since 1964

Television

11 Mar. 2002
BBC 6 Music launches

16 Oct. 2002
1Xtra hits the airwaves

28 Oct. 2002
BBC Asian Network launches
as a national station

15 Dec. 2002
BBC Radio 4 Extra
launches as BBC7

5 Jan. 2013
BBC Local Radio stations begin
a new Saturday evening music
show titled *BBC Introducing*

23 Mar. 2020
BBC Local Radio's *Make
a Difference* campaign
launches during lockdown

1 Nov. 2018
BBC Sounds launches

2000   **2010**   **2020**

26 Mar. 2005
Doctor Who
returns to the air
after 16 years

26 Mar. 2013
BBC Two HD launches;
all remaining channels
are broadcast in HD by
the end of the year

15 May 2004
Strictly Come Dancing
begins its ratings-
beating formula

3 Nov. 2010
BBC One HD
launches

24 Feb. 2019
BBC Scotland
launches

9 Feb. 2003
BBC Three launches

7 Jun. 2020
Michaela Coel's
I May Destroy You
reinvents TV drama

2 Feb. 2002
BBC Four launches

25 Dec. 2007
iPlayer launches

11 Feb. 2002
The channels CBeebies and
CBBC begin broadcasting

BBC RADIO

Covering news, current affairs, culture, arts, business and weather, the first arm of the BBC remains one of its most popular, with a reach that covers the globe. What started out as a single station developed into a network of different platforms, appealing to the widest variety of tastes and interests.

The first BBC radio broadcast took place on 14 November 1922, from Marconi House on London's Strand. It was followed later in the year by broadcasts from Birmingham, Manchester and Newcastle upon Tyne. On 8 January 1923, the first outside broadcast took place, presenting *The Magic Flute* by the British National Opera Company, from Covent Garden. Over the next three years, broadcasts took place from around the United Kingdom. On 7 July 1927, Christopher Stone became the country's first DJ when he presented – dressed in a dinner jacket and tie – a music programme.

Major changes came after the Second World War. The BBC Light Programme (named Radio 2 from 1967) launched on 29 July 1945, offering audiences light music and entertainment. With the remit of engaging with topical and cultural issues, the BBC Third Programme launched on 29 September 1946. It was replaced by Radio 3 in 1967. The BBC Home Service, launched in 1939, became Radio 4 in 1967.

Arguably the biggest shake-up of BBC Radio was the creation of Radio 1 in the late 1960s. It came in answer to the pirate stations that had recently been outlawed, and the creation of the station in 1967 attracted many of those stations' DJs and transformed mainstream radio waves with its focus on current musical trends. Radio 5 launched in 1990, followed by Radio 5 Live in 1994. The early 2000s witnessed an explosion in stations and their variants – including Radio 6 Music – thanks to the arrival of digital broadcasting.

Radio 6 Music duo Stuart Maconie and Mark Radcliffe (above) and Artist in Residence Loyle Carner (right)

THREE COUNTIES

One of the BBC's local radio stations is BBC Three Counties Radio.
Can you use the clues below to work out which three English counties
it covers?

- **All three counties border one another**
- **Two of the county names begin with the same letter**
- **All three county names end with '-shire'**
- **Two of the counties border Cambridgeshire**
  (but Cambridgeshire is not one of the three)
- **One of the county names is only one letter different**
  from a county that borders Wales

LOCAL LEGENDS

Can you match each BBC radio DJ pictured below to the BBC Radio station
that was their local station while they were growing up?

- **BBC Radio Leeds**
- **BBC Radio London**
- **BBC Radio Manchester**
- **BBC Radio Newcastle**
- **BBC Radio Oxford**
- **BBC Radio Scotland**

BBC TELEVISION

Broadcasting at the BBC began in the 1920s, with radio. Within 15 years, television transmissions began. By the late 1950s, it was rapidly gaining ground as the primary medium in everyday life, a position it would continue to hold until the arrival of the Internet.

The BBC's television programming began on 22 August 1932, in the basement of Broadcasting House, just north of Oxford Circus in central London. But it was with the move to Alexandra Palace in north London that regular broadcasts began, from November 1936. These were interrupted by the outbreak of war less than three years later, the broadcaster signing off with a screening of the Mickey Mouse cartoon *Mickey's Gala Premier* (1933). Broadcasting returned on 7 June 1946, and 1964 saw the arrival of the BBC's second channel, BBC Two. Whereas the original

channel catered to a mainstream audience with its mix of current affairs and entertainment, BBC Two's remit was 'to broadcast programmes of depth and substance'.

BBC One and BBC Two would remain the broadcaster's only channels – save for the creation of separate dedicated news and political channels in the 1990s – until the arrival of BBC Four in 2002 and BBC Three in 2003. The former, which ran from 7pm to the early hours of the morning, with daytime programming taken over by CBeebies, was culture driven, with a remit to show a specific amount of new factual, arts and foreign language programming. BBC Three was aimed at a younger, 16- to 34-year-old, audience (and shared time with CBBC). It went online in 2016, but returned to linear television on 1 February 2022.

Raymond Baxter, host of *Tomorrow's World*, which first aired in 1965.
Generations shared his enthusiasm for inventions and gadgets of the future.

MEDIA MATCH

Join each programme or film (on the left) to the BBC channel that first aired it (on the right) by drawing straight lines between the relevant dots. Each line will pass through a letter, and when all of these highlighted letters are then read from top to bottom they will spell out the name of a BBC channel that was later replaced by BBC Four.

Big Cook Little Cook
Eilean Mo Ghaoil
Fireman Sam
Fleabag
Only Connect
Peaky Blinders
Shaun the Sheep
The Papers
The Wrong Trousers

K A M G N U
Z B
O V W
I L R
H D E
T N Q C
G S
E F D
P L J

BBC One
BBC Two
BBC Three
BBC Four
BBC News
BBC Alba
CBBC
CBeebies
S4C

IDENT IDENTITY

Which BBC channels were each of these idents used for? Write your solution in the white space that blocks that channel's name.

Entertainment

From game shows to chat shows and from variety programmes to competitive events, entertainment lies at the heart of the BBC's broadcast schedules. Lord Reith expressed the organization's remit when he outlined that it should 'inform, educate and entertain'. Ever since the broadcaster expanded its radio and television stations, the challenge faced by producers and department heads has been to find the perfect balance of these elements in programming. And to define entertainment for various generations and across all hours of the day. With each new decade tastes have changed and the challenge has widened. What Lord Reith saw as entertainment in the 1920s differs radically to what we enjoy now. After all, it's unlikely he would have envisaged a landscape so wide that it encompassed everything from *Dragons' Den* and *The Voice* to *It's a Knockout* and *RuPaul's Drag Race*.

THE TALK SHOW

A staple of prime-time television programming, the talk show has existed in various guises, running the gamut from the sober and serious to the entertaining and ridiculous. But its format has remained relatively consistent: a host talks to one or more guests, often before a live audience.

The talk show was developed in the United States. Joe Franklin hosted the first in 1951, followed by NBC's *The Tonight Show*, which debuted in 1954 and is today the world's longest-running talk show. In the United Kingdom, where live television programming was a little more formal than in the United States, the relaxed format of the talk show took time to take off. Among the early examples of the interview format was *Face to Face*, a series of acclaimed interviews with figures across the landscape of art, politics, culture, religion and sport.

There have been countless short-lived talk shows, including *Clarkson*, *Davina*, *A Day with Dana*, *The Michael McIntyre Chat Show* and *The Rob Brydon Show*, as well as

parodies of the format such as *The Mrs Merton Show* and *All Round to Mrs Brown's*. But the last 50 years have seen series of shows that won over British audiences, each ending up as one of the BBC's flagship programmes: *Parkinson*, *The Russell Harty Show*, *Wogan*, *Friday Night with Jonathan Ross* and *The Graham Norton Show*. At their best, these shows have successfully balanced humour, insight and intimacy with the element of surprise that comes with filming live.

In 1999, Michael Parkinson interviewed Oprah Winfrey in a solo 50-minute programme. At the time, she was a successful show host in her own right in the United States.

THE GUEST LIST

Each of the A-listers clued below has appeared as a guest on *Parkinson*, with some of them appearing multiple times. Fill in the crossword grid with their surnames by solving the clues. Each clue provides only their first name and their best-known occupation. Who are they all? Once you've filled in the surnames, the letters in the shaded squares can be rearranged to spell out the surname of the guest who has appeared on the show more times than any other.

Across

1. Judi, actor (5)
4. Thierry, footballer (5)
6. Ingrid, actor (7)
7. Tony, politician (5)
8. Peter, comedian (3)
11. Kate, actor (7)
14. Geri, musician (9)
16. Ewan, actor (8)
17. Helen, actor (6)
19. Cameron, actor (4)
21. Ozzy, musician (8)
22. Michael, comedian (5)
23. Jeremy, presenter (8)
24. David, footballer (7)

Down

1. Bette, actor (5)
2. Richard, actor (6)
3. Naomi, model (8)
4. Tom, actor (5)
5. Mel, actor (6)
9. George, musician (7)
10. Daniel, actor (5)
11. Orson, filmmaker (6)
12. Olivia, actor (6-4)
13. Paul, musician (9)
15. Justin, musician (10)
16. Bette, actor (6)
18. Celine, musician (4)
20. Raquel, actor (5)

THE NAME OF THE GAME

Some talk-show hosts are so iconic that they need only one of their names in their show title. In the left-hand column below, six talk-show hosts from eponymous BBC shows have had the name of their show replaced with the other half of their own name. In the right-hand column, the number of episodes of each of these talk shows is given, although the two lists are not in the same order. Can you identify the shows, and match them to the number of episodes that were broadcast?

Black	**8 episodes**
Jeremy	**27 episodes**
McCall	**48 episodes**
Rantzen	**69 episodes**
Terry	**600+ episodes**
Wax	**1,131 episodes**

THE RADIO TIMES

One of the great institutions around the Christmas period, the bumper, two-week festive issue of the *Radio Times* has been a feature in British life for decades. The stalwart publication is nearly as old as the organization whose programme schedules it publishes.

Originally subtitled 'The official organ of the BBC', the *Radio Times* was first published on 28 September 1923. It was created in response to Lord Reith receiving an ultimatum from the Newspaper Publishers Association: unless a fee was paid to newspapers to carry radio listings, the listings would not be published.

Originally the magazine was a joint venture with an external publisher, but the BBC took over editorial control in 1925 and by 1937, the broadcaster was producing the entire publication in house. In 1928, the magazine's remit expanded to include coverage of a regular series of 'experimental television transmissions by the Baird process'. It would become the world's first television listings magazine. By the end of the 1930s, several pages were dedicated to television. After the lean rationing years of the Second World War – which included paper, so the *Radio Times* was reduced in size and produced on wafer-thin pages – the magazine returned to full, detailed coverage and, by 1953, television had moved to the front of the listings.

The recognizable masthead was introduced by editor Geoffrey Cannon at the end of the 1960s. The first full-colour edition was produced in 1990. In February 1991, listings were deregulated, allowing the *Radio Times* and other publications to feature all channels. And in 2021 the wide variety of regional editions, which were first introduced with the 29 July 1945 issue, had been reduced to six large regions.

From the mid-1940s the *Radio Times* was printed a week in advance and liveried lorries and vans distributed it across the country.

SCHEDULE SWITCH

Pictured right are seven of the mastheads that have appeared on the front cover of the *Radio Times* since its inception in the 1930s, given in no particular order. Can you sort the mastheads into chronological order, according to their first appearance? Once sorted, copy the numbers 'n' next to each masthead in that same order into the format n/nn/nnnn. This represents a date in the format day/month/year for which the TV and radio listings were published in two successive issues of the *Radio Times*. Can you guess why?

0

9

0

6

8

THE TEST OF TIMES

Can you answer the following questions about the *Radio Times* and the history of BBC scheduling?

1. **What type of listings disappeared from the *Radio Times* on 3 September 1939 and didn't return until 1946?**
2. **What popular sci-fi show has been the most frequently featured programme on the *Radio Times* cover?**
3. **Until 1957, an hour's gap was scheduled across all TV channels from 6pm to 7pm. What was the hour known as?**
4. **In what year did the *Radio Times* first list the TV schedule before the radio schedule?**
5. **Which BBC channel, which originally began transmitting in 1964, became Britain's first colour TV channel in 1967?**
6. **In what year did BBC Three originally launch as a free-to-air TV channel?**

1

1

VARIETY SHOWS

Variety entertainment had long been a staple of British culture. Music halls, which first appeared in the 1850s, were replaced by the end of the First World War with the more respectable variety shows. This world was replicated in the popular nostalgic series *The Good Old Days*, which ran from 1953–83. But the variety show had already found a home on the small screen before this series first aired.

In 1936, producers Dallas Bower and Harry Pringle developed and produced the show *Cabaret*, which first aired in 1937, ran to the outbreak of the Second World War, and returned for a number of episodes in 1946. It featured many of the most popular performers of the day and was so successful, it led to six spin-off series. Pringle would also produce the Saturday night entertainment *Café Continental*, which ran from 1947–53 and took place on a set designed like a French brasserie. However, the most enduring variety show remains the *Royal Variety Performance*, which was initiated in 1912 (then known as the *Royal Command Performance*) and began airing on television in 1960. It was screened by the BBC until 2010.

Star-driven variety shows became popular from the 1960s, with the host as famous as their guests. The best examples are *The Val Doonican Show*, which ran for 30 years from 1958, the various television shows Shirley Bassey was involved with in the 1960s and 70s, and *Des O'Connor Tonight*, which showed on the BBC from 1977–82. There were also review shows presented by comedians that echoed the format of the variety show, such as those featuring, among others, Les Dawson, Dick Emery, Kenny Everett, John Bishop and Michael McIntyre.

Cliff Richard was among the stars at the first *Royal Variety Performance* to be televised, in 1960. Here, he takes an impressive leap outside the Royal Albert Hall in 1967.

MYSTERY CLUES

Can you solve each of the following clues to reveal six words, one per clue? Then, can you say in what way they are all connected to the *Royal Variety Performance*? The title of this puzzle is also an extra clue . . .

1. **Feeling of good expectation for the future** (4)

2. **Colour of ravens and coal** (5)

3. **Light covering of ice crystals** (5)

4. **Street in Westminster, home to government offices** (9)

5. **High-ranking clergyman** (6)

6. **Male deer** (4)

BITS AND PIECES

Seven types of variety act have been split into bits and pieces below. Can you reassemble all of these pieces to create a typical variety show? Each act will consist of a single word once its components are joined together.

ACR	CE	CO	DAN
DY	GIC	GLI	IC
ISM	JUG	MA	ME
MUS	NG	OBA	OQU
TICS	TRIL	VEN	

THE STARS

Each of the acts pictured below has appeared in the *Royal Variety Performance*. Can you name each band? As a clue, all four band names have something in common.

POPULAR SHOWS

The BBC has always excelled when it comes to entertainment shows that feature a competitive element. Some are aimed at the general family, others cater for a younger audience and have a more educational streak, and others still are laced with humour better suited to the more mature among us.

For younger audiences, one of the longest-running shows was *Top of the Form*. It first broadcast on BBC Light Programme (1948–67) before moving to Radio 2 and then Radio 4 until its cancellation in 1986. It was also a mainstay of BBC One between 1962 and 1975. Older students had the opportunity to compete on *Mastermind*, which ranks alongside *Only Connect* as one of TV's toughest quiz shows.

Some of the most popular shows played to a specific interest base. *A Question of Sport* (1968–) is the longest-running sports quiz show in the world. *Never Mind the Buzzcocks* sought to test the show's celebrity contestants' music knowledge. And *Telly Addicts* tapped into popular culture on the small screen. While *Call My Bluff* and *Would I Lie to You?* saw celebrity panellists attempting to outwit each other, and both *Shooting Stars* and *QI* saw them playfully ridiculed, in *The Weakest Link* and *Pointless* members of the public found themselves tested on their general knowledge as they played a tactical game against each other.

Arguably the most memorable popular entertainment shows tapped into a recipe of humour and competitiveness that held broad appeal. From the absurdity of *It's a Knockout*, the madcap *The Generation Game* and *Blankety Blank* through to the hugely popular *RuPaul's Drag Race*, these shows revel in a playfulness that balances wit with just a little outrage.

Blankety Blank has made a comeback in recent years, with Bradley Walsh as host. Previous hosts include Terry Wogan (above) and Les Dawson (right).

A HOST OF TALENT

Can you match each of the following shows with one of the pictured show hosts? Then, once you have connected each host to a show, can you name the BBC entertainment show that has been hosted by **all four** of the famous faces?

QI

Pointless

Would I Lie to You?

The Weakest Link

1

2

3

4

BLANKETY BLANK

Blanked out to the right are either the first name or surname of ten celebrity panellists on *Blankety Blank*. Fill in the missing names, writing the first letter of each name into the circle provided, and the remainder of each name on the given lines. Once complete, the circles can be read from top to bottom to reveal the name of an iconic *Blankety Blank* host.

◯ _____ Henry

◯ _____ McKellan

Des ◯ _____

Esme ◯ _____

◯ _____ Milligan

◯ _____ Rice

Johnny ◯ _____

◯ _____ Rippon

Gloria ◯ _____

Sophie ◯ _____ -Bextor

RUPAUL'S DRAG RACE

Originally commissioned in 2009 for Logo TV in the United States, as a replacement for the series *Rick & Steve: The Happiest Gay Couple in All the World*, *RuPaul's Drag Race* has become an international success – nowhere more so than in the United Kingdom, where it was an instant hit with its first series.

The show's aim to find 'the United Kingdom's next drag superstar' is carried out via a series of contestant challenges, overseen by four judges, including host RuPaul, along with one guest judge per episode. RuPaul also hosts the show and takes on the role of coach for the contestants. An American drag queen and multi-hyphenate whose hosting of the US edition of the show has won him 11 Primetime Emmy Awards – the most by any person of colour –

RuPaul brings glamour, wit, compassion and, when required, an acerbic tongue to the show.

The format requires contestants to pass a series of stages: a mini challenge, a main challenge, a runway challenge, the judging panel, a lip-synch battle and the elimination of a contestant, which is known as 'sashaying away'. Alongside RuPaul, the judging panel comprises comedians and chat-show hosts Graham Norton and Alan Carr, and Michelle Visage, who was already a hit on the US series. The show's success in the United Kingdom has seen the Australian version of the show, *RuPaul's Drag Race Down Under*, which began airing in May 2021, also screen on the BBC. The comedian Rhys Nicholson joined RuPaul and Michelle Visage as a judge on that series.

From left to right, Michelle Visage, guest judge Oti Mabuse, RuPaul and Alan Carr.

SNATCH MATCH

One of the main challenges in *RuPaul's Drag Race* is the 'Snatch Game', where the queens transform themselves into a celebrity or character of their choosing and impersonate them as if they are contestants on a game show. In the left-hand column below, the first name of a drag queen has been joined with the surname of a celebrity they have impersonated. In the right-hand column the celebrity's first name has been joined with the drag queen's surname. By working out the pairs, can you say who impersonated which celebrity, and then match up each contestant with their picture (right)?

Baga Thatcher
Bimini Price
Ella Lawson
Lawrence Margolyes
Scarlett Culkin
The Trump

Donald Vivienne
Katie Bon Boulash
Macaulay Harlett
Margaret Chipz
Miriam Chaney
Nigella Vaday

1

Queen: _____
Celebrity: _____

2

Queen: _____
Celebrity: _____

3

Queen: _____
Celebrity: _____

4

Queen: _____
Celebrity: _____

5

Queen: _____
Celebrity: _____

6

Queen: _____
Celebrity: _____

LIP-SYNCH

In each episode, two drag queens in danger of elimination must face each other in a 'lip-synch battle', where they both mime to a song to try to save their spot in the competition. Synched up below are the names of four drag queens and songs they have performed on the show, with one pairing per line. Can you separate the pairs of letters, in order to reveal both the songs and the drag queens who 'lip-synched for their lives' to those tracks? Each song and drag queen pair share the same number of letters, but any spaces or punctuation have been ignored.

VH AA LN IL TU CY MI IN AL TA EN

CC AH EL RL YM YL HN OA ML EE

WV IO NU EL GD AI RL SI TE RT OO KY OE US

TT OI AU KC OH MF IE

STRICTLY COME DANCING

There was a time when television audiences might not have been able to tell their quickstep from their tango, an American smooth might have been mistaken for a cocktail and a paso doble a kind of Spanish pudding. A staple of the BBC's autumn scheduling, *Strictly Come Dancing* put paid to those confusions, in recent years becoming one of the most popular competition shows on prime-time BBC One.

Not only that, but Guinness World Records has officially named it the most successful reality television format, its popularity spreading to more than 60 other countries. The format started out, in 1949, as *Come Dancing*. Devised by Eric Morley, the founder of *Miss World*, it was initially geared around two professional dancers, Syd Perkin and Edna Duffield, travelling to regional ballrooms and offering advice and training. It became a competition-driven show in 1953. Entrants to the show would have already had significant experience on the dancefloor circuit. This version of the show remained on air until 1998.

It was then relaunched in its celebrity-driven format in 2004 by Richard Hopkins, who was behind the British launch of Channel 4's *Big Brother*. The show's title was a combination of the previous series and Baz Luhrmann's hit movie *Strictly Ballroom* (1992). The show was originally presented by Bruce Forsyth and Tess Daly, with Claudia Winkleman coming on board following Forsyth's retirement in 2014. Three judges – the longest standing of whom is Craig Revel Horwood – and an audience phone poll decide which dancing couple make it through to the next round. The winners often display a combination of charisma, skill and hell-for-leather determination.

Entertainer Bruce Forsyth was known for his dance moves and catchphrases. At the end of *Strictly* he and Tess Daly urged viewers to 'Keeeeep dancing'.

WINNER, WINNER

The names of eight *Strictly Come Dancing* winners have each been partnered with the name of a ballroom dance below. Each name has its letters in the correct order, but it's up to you to work out how the two have become intertwined. All spaces have been removed.

1. NQAUTIASCHKASKTAEPLINSPKY

2. ADRARGENRETINENTGOANUGHGO

3. AMMAERKRICRAMANPSRMAOKOATHSH

4. AFLEOSHXADITRXONOT

5. LOSUIASMSMBITAH

6. CHABABCEHYACLCANHCYA

7. SPTAASCOEDYODBOLOELEY

8. KVIEENLNVEISNEFWLAELTCTHZER

SCORES ON THE DOORS

The names of nine *Strictly Come Dancing* judges have each been assigned a score from 2 to 10 inclusive, and then their names have been disguised according to that score. The score determines how many places forward through the alphabet a judge's name has been shifted. For example, if guest judge Jennifer Grey had a score of '1' then all of the letters of her name would have been shifted one place forward in the alphabet so that J became K, e became f, n became o and so on, giving the result 'Kfoojgfs Hsfz'. Letters 'wrap around' from the end of the alphabet to the start.

Who are the hidden judges and what are their scores? Which one has scored the highest?

A. Etcki Tgxgn Jqtyqqf

B. Slu Nvvkthu

C. Fwqjsj Umnqqnux

D. Itmapi Lqfwv

E. Jgxike Hayykrr

F. Wlmvpic Feppew

G. Vxcbr Vjkdbn

H. Dqwrq Gx Ehnh

I. Lbexy Dyxsyvs

DRAGONS' DEN

The business equivalent of a gladiatorial ring, with a sizeable television audience cheering on the underdogs, while also baying for at least a little corporate blood, *Dragons' Den* has become an international success.

First created in Japan under the title *Money Tigers*, versions of the show have appeared in Afghanistan, Austria, China, Colombia, Finland, Russia, Slovenia and Sri Lanka, where it is known respectively as, *Dream and Achieve*, *2 Minutes 2 Million*, *Chinese Partner*, *Shark Tank* (also the name of the US version), *Lion's Mouth*, *Kapital*, *Good Deal* and *Wall of Tuskers*.

Broadcast for three years from 2001 in Japan, the format was purchased from Sony Pictures Television by BBC Manchester and first aired on BBC Two on 4 January 2005, with economist and political journalist Evan Davis remaining its sole presenter.

In each episode, contestants needing financial backing and expertise present their case to five entrepreneurs. The contestant has to specify the amount they require and if they are unsuccessful in raising this amount or more, they leave with nothing. In return, the investors – more than one can pledge money towards a specific business – demand equity as part of the deal.

The original series featured 'dragons' Peter Jones, Rachel Elnaugh, Doug Richard, Simon Woodroffe and Duncan Bannatyne. Jones is the only member to have remained on board for all subsequent series, with Bannatyne, Deborah Meaden, Theo Paphitis, James Caan and Touker Suleyman being the show's other longest-running and most recognizable investors. Each is notable for their unwillingness to suffer either fools or the badly prepared.

Legendary Dragons, from left to right, James Caan, Duncan Bannatyne, Theo Paphitis, Deborah Meaden and Peter Jones.

TORN TO SHREDS

The names of five products brought in front of the Dragons have been torn into shreds (right). All five products failed to gain any investment on the show, but have since gone on to become household names. Can you put the pieces back together, and reveal which opportunities the Dragons missed out on? Any spaces or punctuation in their names have been ignored.

ATI	BR	CU	DES
ETEE	EWD	NE	NGL
NKI	OG	ON	PAWI
TA	TIN	TRU	ZER

A SLICE OF THE PIE

Some products and businesses are lucky enough to attract the investment of more than one Dragon, who each want their own slice of the pie. Sliced up below are the names of companies that gained investment from two or more Dragons on the programme. Can you work out how you would put the pie back together and therefore find 14 businesses that pitched their way to success?

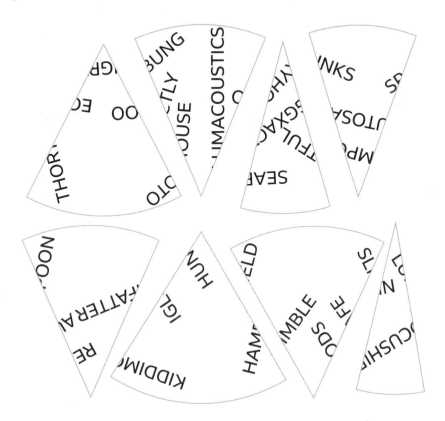

TOP GEAR

The televisual Valhalla for petrolheads, *Top Gear* has driven its way to extraordinary success. The programme has so far existed as three very distinct models, with an overall lifespan that has grown far beyond the modest aims of its creator, who pitched his original idea about cars, highways and road safety to BBC Midlands in 1977.

Created by producer Derek Smith, *Top Gear* first aired in the Midlands region for just nine monthly episodes, presented by local newscaster Tom Coyne and national *Nine O'Clock News* presenter Angela Rippon. The show was a success and, the following year, the BBC commissioned ten episodes for national broadcast. By 1980, the show had proven popular enough with audiences for it to be part of BBC Two's regular programming, with two series per year, covering late winter/early spring, then returning for autumn/early winter. Topics ran the gamut, from overviews of the latest cars, the shifting nature of traffic around the country and a focus on special events from races to motor shows. Hosts over the years include Sue Barker, Noel Edmonds, Kate Humble, Stirling Moss, James May and Jeremy Clarkson.

Clarkson, along with producer Andy Wilman, oversaw a reformatted show in 2002, following its cancellation by the BBC in 2001. The former fronted it, with Richard Hammond and Jason Dawe, who was replaced a year later by May. It proved hugely successful, becoming more celebrity driven and involving audience participation. Following a series of controversial incidents, the BBC reshuffled the format and brought in new presenters, first with Chris Evans and Matt LeBlanc, then with former cricketer Andrew Flintoff and Paddy McGuinness.

With his identity kept secret, The Stig coached guest celebrities in negotiating a racetrack at top speed in a 'reasonably priced car'.

THE MYSTERIOUS STIG

The Stig is a mysterious driver who has appeared on several series of *Top Gear*, and whose name – and face – are shrouded in mystery, as one of the programme's running jokes. But never mind about their identity – can you even *find* The Stig? To do so, spell out 'The Stig' by starting on any roundabout labelled with a 'T' and then following the roads to adjacent roundabouts. You can't visit any roundabout more than once. How quickly can you find him?

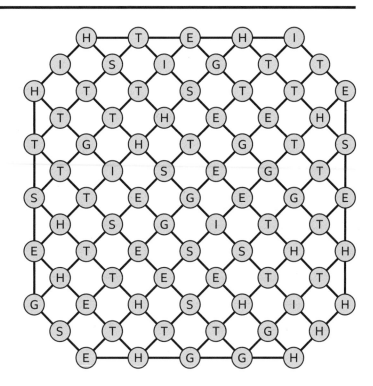

DRIVERS AND RIDES

The surnames of eight Formula 1 racing drivers who have appeared on *Top Gear* have each been paired with a make of car below that has the same number of letters as their name, ignoring any spaces. For each letter pair, assign one letter to the driver and one letter to the car. Who are the drivers? What are the makes of car?

1. RC HI EC VC IR AO LR DE TO

2. HM EA RM IC LE DT OE SN

3. VN EI TS ST AE LN

4. LB AA RM BR OI CR HG HE LI NL OI

5. TB OU YT TO TO NA

6. AR LA FI AK RK OO MN EE NO

7. FH IO LR DL

8. SV OC LH UK MS AW CA GH EE NR

THE APPRENTICE

One of the most popular and successful reality competition formats, *The Apprentice* made its debut on US television in 2004 and within a year its British counterpart screened on the BBC. A competition to find the most successful business candidate out of a wide range of entrants, it has seen winners enjoy a fair degree of success and, in some cases, notoriety.

Created by British television producer Mark Burnett, the US series was hosted by Donald Trump for 14 seasons, before his entry into the US political arena. In the UK version, Trump's mantle was taken by business magnate Alan Sugar. The show originally aired on BBC Two, but its runaway success saw it win a prime-time slot on BBC One after two seasons.

The show appears to take place over consecutive weeks, but is actually filmed over a period of two months before the first episode is aired. In each episode, Sugar sets a team-oriented task to test each individual's business acumen, abilities as a salesperson, leadership skills and their adaptability in dealing with people. Upon completion of each task, the candidates return to Sugar's boardroom, where he and his advisers assess the success of what has been achieved and the individual performance of each person. At the end of each episode a contestant is removed from the series with the words 'You're fired'.

Almost two decades into its run, the show remains popular with audiences and has made celebrities of a number of its contestants and advisers, while establishing Sugar as a household name. But unlike his American counterpart, Sugar has so far shown no interest in entering the political arena.

Lord Alan Sugar (centre right), with advisers Nick Hewer and Margaret Mountford (left) and Adrian Chiles (far right), presenter of companion show *The Apprentice: You're Fired!*

SPORT RELIEF

In 2018, a one-off special of *The Apprentice* was created for *Sport Relief*, with ten celebrity contestants competing against one another. On each line below the surname of one of these celebrity contestants has been blended with an Olympic sport by taking alternate letters from each name. For example, KOHLI and RUGBY could be blended to give KUHBI by taking the first, third and final letters of KOHLI and the second and fourth letters of RUGBY. Use the letters and the clues to find out which celebrities and sports have been combined below.

1. **BRLHIRG**
   BBC sports presenter, including of *Sport Relief* and the Olympic Games

2. **FANCICG**
   Original presenter of sports quiz *They Think It's All Over*

3. **RODTNAPL**
   Singer and 2016 *Strictly Come Dancing* finalist

4. **SUINILG**
   Cricketer and long-running captain on *A Question of Sport*

SLIPPERY SLOPE

There can be a fine line between winning and losing. Link one to the other by solving each of the following clues, writing one letter per gap.

_ I R E D	If you win *The Apprentice*, you are _____
_ _ I R E D	Joined into twos
_ _ _ I R E D	Presided over a meeting
_ _ _ _ I R E D	Filled with self-belief
_ _ _ _ _ I R E D	Had the opposite effect of that intended
_ _ _ _ I R E D	Bought
_ _ _ I R E D	Ceased working
_ _ I R E D	Having a conical tower, as a church
_ I R E D	If you lose *The Apprentice*, you are _____

Drama

Drama has come a long way since it first became a part of the BBC's programming schedule. An adaptation of Luigi Pirandello's short play *The Man with the Flower in his Mouth* was broadcast live on 14 July 1930 to the select few who then owned a television. Some radio dramas were even older, but the earliest surviving recording is of Sir Christopher Wren, broadcast on 20 October 1932. Since then, drama has flourished in all forms. Radio plays and adaptations remain popular, while television encompasses all walks of our daily lives, reaches into the near and distant past, and frequently visits imagined realities years from now. It has produced children's classics, visualized the worlds of Austen, Dickens, Thackeray and the Brontës, and offers a window on to worlds that vary from our own. From the doomsday threat of *Edge of Darkness* and the swooning romance of *Pride and Prejudice* to the complexities of modern life in *I May Destroy You*, drama gives voice to our fears, desires, angst and emotion.

COSTUME DRAMA

Attracting success around the world, the costume drama has rarely been out of favour with audiences, whether inspired by literature or evoking periods of British history – especially the characterful Tudors.

Period dramas had been popular on radio in the 1930s, but it was from the late 1960s that their success on television grew. And it was not long before the costume drama came to represent fictional recreations of the period beginning in the Georgian era and ending around the 1930s. It is no surprise, then, that the works of Jane Austen, George Eliot, Elizabeth Gaskell, Anthony Trollope, Charlotte and Emily Brönte and Charles Dickens became perfect source material. And to international audiences they came to represent a certain kind of Britishness.

Scenes from the BBC's costume dramas, *The Six Wives of Henry VIII* (above) and *I, Claudius* (right).

Alongside adaptations of well-known British literature came other costume dramas. *Upstairs Downstairs*, which ran from 1971–75 (and returned for two series from 2010–12), was hugely popular and would pave the way for series such as *The Onedin Line*, *When the Boat Comes In* and *Poldark*, the latter gripping the nation not once, but twice, in 1975 and 2015.

Of the landmark series, there is the acclaimed 1976 adaptation of Robert Graves' *I, Claudius*, which set the standard for intelligent, involving costume drama. A 2005 take on *Bleak House*, unfolding over 15 half-hour episodes, revitalized Dickens for a modern audience, while losing none of its complexity. And *Peaky Blinders* presented an alternative history of early 20th-century Britain. But few costume dramas have been as admired and beloved by audiences as Andrew Davies' 1995 adaptation of *Pride and Prejudice*.

THE CHRONOLOGY OF COSTUME

Each of the images below comes from a well-known BBC costume drama. Can you order the images chronologically, by the period they depict? To help you, the names of the shows have been given below – although not necessarily in the same order.

Once the images are in the correct order, the letters in the bottom left-hand corner of each image can be read to reveal the name of the main character in the most 'modern' of these series. Who is this character?

- *Ashes to Ashes*
- *Call the Midwife*
- *Gentleman Jack*
- *I, Claudius*
- *Life on Mars*
- *North and South*
- *Poldark*
- *Upstairs, Downstairs*
- *Wolf Hall*

THE ART AND THE ARTIST

On each line opposite, an item of period clothing has been blended with the surname of a writer of a book or play that has been adapted into a costume drama by the BBC. The names and clothing items each have their letters in the correct order, but it's up to you to work out how they've been blended together. Can you identify them all?

1. PBRUISESTLTELEY
2. DFOIUELBDLIENTG
3. THOCMOPRSESTON
4. BFOLANUNBETERT
5. PSETHTICAOWAT
6. HBRAERECDHEYS
7. WCHIELMIDESE
8. HBOUDGICOE

PRIDE AND PREJUDICE

What makes a classic drama? Whatever the ingredients, the combination of Jane Austen, Andrew Davies' sublime adaptation, Jennifer Ehle, a famously shirtless Colin Firth and some of England's most lush, verdant scenery added up to a landmark series, the popularity of which has rarely waned since it first aired on BBC One in September and October 1995.

Jane Austen published *Pride and Prejudice*, a Regency romance with shades of satire, in 1813. Detailing the combative relationship between Elizabeth Bennet and Mr Darcy, it was first adapted as a stage play, then for cinema, before finally reaching the small screen. A 1936 stage version was the basis of the 1940 Academy Award-winning big-screen adaptation starring Greer Garson and Laurence Olivier, which remained arguably the most famous adaptation until the 1990s and the BBC adaptation.

Casting of the two leads in Simon Langton's production – the BBC's fifth adaptation of the novel – determined the rest of the cast. Jennifer Ehle was chosen from six potential actors, while producer Sue Birtwistle was determined to cast the then little-known Colin Firth, who was reticent to play a period role and only accepted after turning it down a number of times. The couple's chemistry chimed with Davies' shifting of the drama from the uniquely female to the male perspective too, along with an emphasis on money during this era.

Lacock in Wiltshire and Lyme Hall in Cheshire were two of the key locations chosen for filming, the latter witnessing Darcy's emerging from a lake that made Firth a star. But the series as a whole has come to represent BBC period drama at its very best: intelligent, witty, moving and visually ravishing.

(Above) Ehle and Firth in the roles of Elizabeth Bennet and Mr Darcy in 1995; (right) a 1952 BBC production, starring Prunella Scales.

THE PERFECT MATCH

Each of the lines below is spoken by either Elizabeth Bennet or Mr Darcy in the BBC adaptation of *Pride and Prejudice* – but can you say which character spoke each line?

1. 'After abusing you so abominably to your face, I could have no scruple in abusing you to all your relations.'
2. 'From the very beginning, your manners impressed me with the fullest belief of your arrogance, your conceit and your selfish distain for the feelings of others.'
3. 'I fear I am ill-qualified to recommend myself to strangers.'
4. 'I have never desired your good opinion and you have certainly bestowed it most unwillingly.'
5. 'I know you find great enjoyment in professing opinions which are not your own.'
6. 'In vain I have struggled. It will not do. My feelings will not be repressed. You must allow me to tell you how ardently I admire and love you.'
7. 'My courage always rises with every attempt to intimidate me.'
8. 'You are too generous to trifle with me. If your feelings are what they were last April, tell me so at once.'
9. 'Your good opinion is rarely bestowed, and therefore more worth the earning.'

FACE TO FACE

Each of these characters (eventually!) forms one half of a couple in *Pride and Prejudice*, but their names have been encoded by shifting each letter a fixed number of positions forward through the alphabet. MR BENNET shifted one place, for example, becomes NS CFOOFU, where M has become N, R has become S, B has become C, and so on. Characters in each couple have had their names shifted by the same amount, and furthermore each couple has been shifted by a different number of letters according to the order of their engagements in the story. Which couples become engaged, and in what order?

NAFKC DGPPGV

JMXDAMPPMEQ HEVGC

IGQTIG YKEMJCO

DIBSMPUUF MVDBT

MDQH EHQQHW

IPMDEFIXL FIRRIX

XJMMJBN DPMMJOT

FKDUOHV ELQJOHB

LANDMARK DRAMA

Original drama, alongside its costume equivalent, has played a crucial element across the history of the BBC's television output. And from the 1950s on, the broadcaster was responsible for programmes that not only attracted acclaim, both at home and internationally, but launched the careers of countless writers and filmmakers. They set a high standard for what the television drama could engage with and achieve. And they were frequently seen as a barometer of the nation's social, political and moral health.

If pre-war dramas were little more than filmed theatre, the 1950s saw a steady stream of popular shows. Anthology series such as *The Wednesday Play*, *Theatre 625* and *Play for Today* were hugely influential, as were one-off productions such as Peter Watkins' remarkable docudrama *Culloden*. But drama eventually came to dominate programming. Landmark series include Alan Bleasdale's *Boys from the Blackstuff*, *Edge of Darkness*, Dennis Potter's *Pennies from Heaven* and *The Singing Detective*, the scabrously funny *Tutti Frutti* and Alan Bennett's acclaimed series of monologues, *Talking Heads*.

Subsequent notable dramas range from the political satire *House of Cards* and the decades-spanning *Our Friends in the North* to the zeitgeisty twentysomething series *This Life*. And in the 2000s, if the kinetic style of *Line of Duty* and *Bodyguard* proved influential over a range of contemporary dramas, Michaela Coel's *I May Destroy You* felt like it broke new ground in every way imaginable.

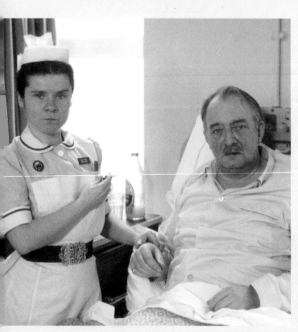

Scenes from the landmark dramas *The Singing Detective* (left) and *Boys from the Blackstuff* (right).

OUR FRIENDS IN THE NORTH

Set in Newcastle, *Our Friends in the North* launched the careers of these four famous faces. Can you name each of the actors pictured below, and then match each actor with two of the further BBC shows listed, which they have also appeared in or narrated?

- *Bodyguard*
- *Copenhagen*
- *Doctor Who*
- *Saint-Ex*

- *The A Word*
- *The Long Firm*
- *The Silence*
- *Who Do You Think You Are?*

1

2

3

4

TALKING HEADS

Episode titles from Alan Bennett's landmark series *Talking Heads* are listed below, though the final word in each title has been replaced with a crossword-style clue. Can you solve the clues, complete the titles and then fit the final words into the grid below, one letter per box?

1. A Woman of No **Significance or value** (10)
2. A Chip in the **Opposite of sour** (5)
3. A Lady of **Enveloped communications** (7)
4. Bed Among the **Pulses found in soups and stews** (7)
5. Her Big **Opportunity** (6)
6. A Cream Cracker Under the **Sofa** (6)
7. Miss Fozzard Finds Her **Body parts you stand on** (4)
8. The Hand of **A deity** (3)
9. Playing **Bread-surrounded food items** (10)
10. The Outside **Canine** (3)
11. Nights in the Gardens of **An Iberian country** (5)
12. Waiting for the **Message sent by telegraph** (8)
13. An ordinary **Adult female** (5)
14. The **Venerated tomb of a saint, perhaps** (6)

PLAY FOR TODAY

From the mid-1960s, the broadcaster embarked on a number of consecutive anthology drama series that introduced a new generation of creative talent who would have a huge influence over BBC drama in the coming decades. *The Wednesday Play*, which ran from 1964–70, set the stage, with such influential productions as Ken Loach's adaptations of Nell Dunn's *Up the Junction* (1965) and *Cathy Come Home* (1966), and Peter Watkin's *The War Game* (1966), whose controversial subject matter delayed its appearance on television until the 1980s.

The Wednesday Play was succeeded by *Play for Today*, which ran from 1970–84. Graeme MacDonald and Irene Shubik, who created the former, were transferred to the new series, which featured works by a new generation of writers and directors who would come to

dominate British drama on stage, as well as on the large and small screen. Writers included Ian McEwan, John Osborne, Dennis Potter, Stephen Poliakoff, David Hare, Willy Russell, Alan Bleasdale, David Storey and Andrew Davies. Among the directors were Stephen Frears, Alan Clarke, Michael Apted, Mike Newell, Roland Joffé, Ken Loach, Lindsay Anderson and Mike Leigh. The last featured adaptations of his successful stage plays *Nuts in May* (1976) and *Abigail's Party* (1977), cementing his career.

Alan Bleasdale's *The Black Stuff*, which screened in 1980, eventually became a landmark polemical drama series, while Dennis Potter's *Brimstone & Treacle* is arguably the broadcaster's most controversial production. The series was eventually replaced by *Screen Two* and *Screen One*.

(Above) A scene from *The Long Distance Piano Player* (1970); (top right) Anthony Hopkins in *Hearts and Flowers* (1970).

PLAY FOR YESTERDAY

In the crossword below, each of the clued solutions is the name of a one-word play that featured on *Play for Today*. Once the puzzle is complete, the letters in the highlighted boxes can be rearranged to spell out the two-word name (6, 3) of the BBC programme that later took over the transmission of single dramas. What is it?

Across

4. Male monarch (4)
6. Beatles song, "Hey ___" (4)
7. Choice to turn off a Windows computer (8)
8. Titled women (6)
9. Large bovines (4)
10. Simone, Wadia or Conti (4)
14. US First Lady, ___ Roosevelt (7)
16. Carpet-like green plant (4)
17. Abode (4)
18. Friend, informally (3)
19. Nation (7)
20. Apologetic (5)

Down

1. *Brideshead Revisited* author, ___ Waugh (6)
2. J, Ware or Wallace (6)
3. Dirty froth (4)
5. Mobsters (9)
11. Lungful of air (6)
12. Demonstration or march (7)
13. Fate (7)
15. Small child, informally (6)

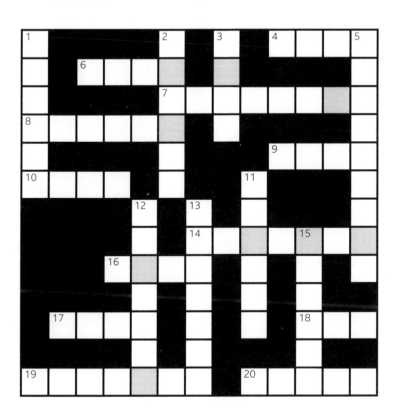

EDGE OF DARKNESS

By the mid-1980s, escalating hostilities between the United States and the Soviet Union, the deployment of nuclear arms at the US base at Greenham Common, and the women-led movement that rose up in opposition to it, saw the rise in fears over a possible nuclear conflict.

Secrecy surrounding how these arms were transported around the United Kingdom increased interest in environmentalist James Lovelock's Gaia hypotheses and the shady role played by corporations all fed into Troy Kennedy Martin's six-part series, which aired to great acclaim in 1985, setting a high watermark for limited drama series.

When the daughter of Yorkshire police detective Ronald Craven (Bob Peck) is killed in what appears to be an assassination attempt on his own life by an IRA hitman – a reprisal for his once being stationed in Northern Ireland – few

questions are asked. But Craven's uncovering of his daughter's role as an anti-nuclear activist soon has him investigating the murky world of the UK's nuclear defence industry and the cover-up of what could have been a major disaster. But his investigation also poses a threat to his own life and anyone who helps him.

Drawing on the conspiracy thrillers popular in 1970s Hollywood, Martin's drama, directed by Martin Campbell, proved a huge success, both critically and with audiences. Eschewing a more kinetic style that Campbell would later employ in a film career that encompassed the Bond films *Goldeneye* (1995) and *Casino Royale* (2006), as well as *The Legend of Zorro* (2005) and the superfluous 2010 Hollywood remake of this series, *Edge of Darkness* was all the more plausible for its understated approach to the material.

Bob Peck in the lead role as police detective Ronald Craven and Joanne Whalley as his daughter, Emma.

HIDING IN THE SHADOWS

Can you add a central word to each of the pairs below, to form two common English phrases? One phrase consists of the first and centre word, and the other phrase consists of the centre and last word. The number of letters is shown by the underscore marks. For example, NUCLEAR _ _ _ _ _ STRUGGLE is solved with 'POWER', to create NUCLEAR POWER and POWER STRUGGLE.

Once complete, read down the list of revealed words from top to bottom to uncover more information about *Edge of Darkness*.

1. COMMON   _ _ _ _   FRAME
2. CIVIL   _ _ _   ZONE
3. PIPING   _ _ _   TICKET
4. BRAIN   _ _ _ _   BLOCK
5. BREAK   _ _ _ _ _   STORY
6. BUCKLE   _ _   STICKS

UNCOVERED UNFORTUNATELY

Hidden below is the name of something Craven uncovers in his investigation – something that should be kept concealed. To reveal it, write a word on each line, with one letter per box. A clue to the meaning of each word is given, and all of the words use just eight different letters between them. Further, each letter has been replaced by a different number. Once you have cracked the number code, you can reveal what Craven finds in his investigation. This hidden item is indicated by the arrow.

Locate with precision

1	7	6	1	5	7	6	4

Instinct

7	6	4	3	7	4	7	5	6

Maximum value

2	7	8	7	4

Environmental damage

1	5	2	2	3	4	7	5	6

→

1	2	3	4	5	6	7	3	8

I MAY DESTROY YOU

Michaela Coel's groundbreaking series aired in the wake of #MeToo and Black Lives Matter. It confronts sexual assault, racism, misogyny, patriarchy, the vagaries of social media, and personal relationships.

Aside from the glaring absence of nominations at certain awards – evidence of the very prejudice that the show was highlighting – *I May Destroy You* received numerous accolades, at home and abroad. It is arguably one of the most significant television dramas of its era.

Coel, who also wrote, co-directed and executive produced the show, plays Arabella, a gifted Twitter star whose book *Chronicles of a Fed-Up Millennial* saw her proclaimed the voice of a generation. However, she finds herself struggling with her follow-up title. Moreover, she is haunted by the barely remembered events of a night out with her friends. Gradually recalling she had been drugged then sexually assaulted, Arabella finds her life going into tailspin, exacerbated by additional events and revelations in the life of her friends Terry (Weruche Opia) and Kwame (Paapa Essiedu).

Coel had already garnered acclaim for her previous series *Chewing Gum*. And it was while working on that show that she was sexually assaulted. Although this was the basis of *I May Destroy You*, the show targets a wide range of issues, never afraid to challenge injustice, but also eschews easy answers in favour of acknowledging how complex our mediated lives are. Moving between Arabella's past and present, the drama builds towards a brilliant, surprising final episode that finds Arabella reconciling with events that have irrevocably changed her and showing unwilling to be weighed down by them.

Michaela Cole in the lead role as writer Arabella Essiedu, in a drama that is by turns dense, disturbing, moving, funny and provocative.

CHARACTER FIT

All of these characters from *I May Destroy You* can be placed into the grid below, with one letter per square, except for one. The name that does not fit is the name of the show's main antagonist. Who is it?

3-letter names
BEN
KAI
KAT

4-letter names
JACK
KOJO
RUMI
RYAN

5-letter names
DAMON
DAVID
EMILY
JAMAL
KWAME
LUIGI
MALIK
SIMON
TARIQ
TERRY

6-letter names
ALISSA
BISOLA
JULIAN
LENORA
SAMSON
TYRONE

7-letter names
CHISARA
LORETTA

8-letter names
ARABELLA
FRANCINE
MATHILDA

SOCIAL MUDDLE

The names of seven popular social media platforms have been jumbled up (right), with one per line. In addition, one extra letter has been added to each name. When these extra letters are removed and read in order, the name of a final social media channel featured in *I May Destroy You* will be revealed. Can you identify all of the social media platforms?

ACT OF OK BE (8)
A WARM STING (9)
CASH PAINT (8)
IT TO KKT (3, 3)
PRETTIEST N (9)
PAW THE SAP (8)
OUTER BUY (7)

THE CRIME DRAMA

When it comes to entertainment, crime has always paid handsomely. The vicarious thrill of illicit underworld activities and the work of law enforcement in combatting them has kept audiences enthralled, from daytime dramas through to prime-time entertainment, and from the distant past to the here and now.

The sheer number of crime series and one-off dramas that have thrilled over the years would fill a large volume of its own. But there have been standout achievements and beloved favourites over the decades.

How the forces of law and order have been represented can be seen as a reflection of societal mores of the time. For instance, *Dixon of Dock Green*, which began airing in 1955, depicted the police as the bulwark of society. Even Queen Elizabeth II, visiting the studios

where it was filmed, commented that the series had 'become part of the British way of life'. This trend continued in subsequent series such as *Z-Cars*, which first appeared in 1962, *Juliet Bravo*, which first aired in 1980 and placed a female officer in a lead role, *Bergerac* (1981) and *Death in Paradise* (2011). Other series, from *Between the Lines*, *Silent Witness*, *Luther* and *Line of Duty* to *The Fall*, *Happy Valley* and *Vigil* have strayed further into morally ambiguous territory.

The private detective has always had more freedom in terms of colourful characterization, whether Joan Hickson's beloved portrayal of Miss Marple between 1984 and 1992, Trevor Eve's Eddie Shoestring (1979), Alan Davies' Jonathan Creek (1997) or Benedict Cumberbatch's singular Sherlock (2010).

Benedict Cumberbatch (left) and Martin Freeman (right), as Sherlock Holmes and his loyal friend, Doctor John Watson.

CRIME SCENES

Each of the BBC crime dramas clued below is set somewhere in the United Kingdom, or just off-shore. Each series name has been disguised, however, by removing any letters also found in the word 'CRIME'. For example, 'THE RESPONDER' would have become 'TH SPOND'.

Can you first identify the nine crime dramas, then match each of them to the point on the map that marks the location where the first series of each show was set? Although, to make this second stage trickier, any letters also found in the word 'SCENE' have been removed from the map labels.

1. **BGA**
2. **HAPPY VALLY**
3. **HDDN**
4. **HOP STT**
5. **LUTH**
6. **PAKY BLNDS**
7. **SLNT WTNSS**
8. **TH SSNG**
9. **VGL**

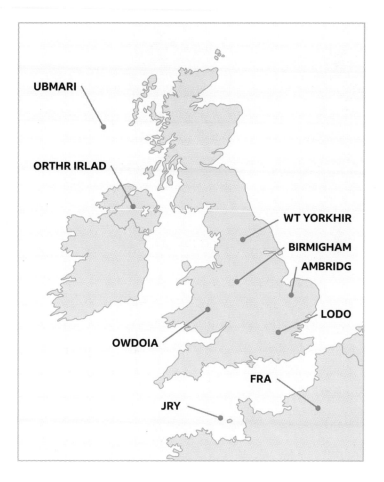

UBMARI

ORTHR IRLAD

WT YORKHIR

BIRMIGHAM

AMBRIDG

LODO

OWDOIA

FRA

JRY

PEAKY BLINDERS

A hyper-violent, stylized drama set in early 20th-century Birmingham with a contemporary soundtrack might not appear, on paper, to be a likely recipe for success. But this tale of the Shelby family's rise through British society and the ranks of its underworld has not only proved a winner with domestic audiences, it has gained an ecstatic and loyal international following.

Peaky Blinders was the creation of Steven Knight, who was the screenwriter of *Dirty Pretty Things* (2002) and *Eastern Promises* (2007), and the writer-director of *Hummingbird* (2007) and *Locke* (2013). Born and raised in Birmingham, he has stated that his influences for the series were a combination of childhood stories about the region's criminal past and the Western genre.

Knight's intention was to create 'a story of a family between two wars, and by ending it with the first air-raid siren in Birmingham'. The narrative revolves around the exploits of Thomas 'Tommy' Shelby (Cillian Murphy), his matriarchal sister Elizabeth or 'Polly' (Helen McCrory) and psychotic brother Arthur (Paul Anderson), as well as members of their extended family and the various gangs they encounter, from Tom Hardy's Jewish boss in London to Adrien Brody's Italian mobster from New York. Although the series' main characters are fictional, *Peaky Blinders* hews closely to British history from this period and features actual characters such as Winston Churchill and Oswald Mosley.

The show's impressive production values and performances, combined with kinetic direction, action set-pieces and plotting that keeps audiences on a knife-edge of suspense, proved irresistible. But *Peaky Blinders* also stands out for its originality, taking the gangster genre into new territory with no small amount of verve.

Irish actor Cillian Murphy plays the fierce gangland boss Tommy Shelby, known for his cold, hard stare.

FAMILY TIES

Can you use your skills of logical deduction to complete the Shelby family tree? Siblings and half-siblings are placed in order of birth from first (left) to last (right). Not all spouses and children mentioned on the show are included in the tree, but all the information you need to match each name to a number in the tree is given.

- **Ada Shelby is the fourth of five siblings**
- **Ada Shelby is Arthur Shelby Sr's daughter**
- **Arthur Shelby Jr has one child, Billy**
- **Elizabeth Shelby and Arthur Shelby Sr are siblings**
- **Elizabeth Shelby is Arthur Shelby Jr's aunt**
- **Esme Lee is Finn Shelby's sister-in-law**
- **Finn Shelby has no spouse, or children**
- **Finn Shelby is Karl Thorne's uncle**
- **Freddie Thorne is Karl Thorne's father**
- **Gina Gray is Elizabeth Shelby's daughter-in-law**
- **Grace Burgess is Charles Shelby's mother**
- **John Shelby is the middle of five siblings**
- **Linda Shelby married the eldest of five Shelby siblings**
- **Lizzie Stark's daughter is Ruby Shelby**
- **Michael Gray and John Shelby are first cousins**
- **Ruby Shelby is Martha Strong's granddaughter**
- **Thomas Shelby has been married twice, and has a daughter and a son**
- **Tommy Shelby's first child was a boy**

NAMES TO PLACE:
Ada Shelby
Arthur Shelby Jr
Arthur Shelby Sr
Billy Shelby
Charles Shelby
Elizabeth Shelby
Esme Lee
Finn Shelby
Freddie Thorne
Gina Gray
Grace Burgess
John Shelby
Karl Thorne
Linda Shelby
Lizzie Stark
Martha Strong
Michael Gray
Ruby Shelby
Thomas Shelby

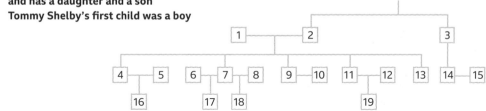

TARGET PRACTICE

Can you find all of the clued words in the circle below? Each letter can be used no more than once per answer, and every word must use the central letter. There is also one unclued word that uses all of the letters exactly once, and which describes the official occupation of several Shelby family members. What is it?

In a frenzied fashion, as in 'to run ____' (4)
Cartoon explosion sound (6)
Steal property from (3)
Penniless, informally (5)
Gang (3)
Travel aimlessly (4)

ACTION, MYTH, ADVENTURE

Worlds of myth and epic quests have long been a staple of the large and small screen. But the development of increasingly sophisticated special and visual effects, and the introduction of digital technology, have given these worlds greater scope.

An early example of the BBC drama department branching out into the adventure format was *Adam Adamant Lives!*, which aired over two series from 1966. It was a satirical look at the 1960s through the perspective of an Edwardian adventurer who had been frozen in the late 19th century. A more sedate form of adventure was experienced by three siblings in *The Railway Children*, whose popularity led to a 1970 film version, with both starring Jenny Agutter.

Magical worlds could be found in the acclaimed 1984 adaptation of John Masefield's 1935 children's classic *The Box of Delights*, and *Jonathan Strange & Mr Norrell*, an adaptation of

Susanna Clarke's alternative history of Europe at the time of the Napoleonic wars and the machinations of two gifted magicians. A secret world in London was also the topic of Neil Gaiman and Lenny Henry's *Neverwhere*, while the alternate universe of Philip Pullman's *His Dark Materials* trilogy began airing in 2019.

The 2000s saw increasing interest in mythic or fictional figures. *Merlin* proved to be a huge hit, with audiences drawn to its blend of myth and history. It was followed by *Atlantis* and the revival of Alexandre Dumas' classic tale of derring-do in *The Musketeers*.

(Left) Hugo Speer and Luke Pasqualino star in *The Musketeers*; (right) Jenny Agutter in *The Railway Children*.

OTHER-WORLDLY EXPERIENCES

The left-hand column below contains the disguised names of eight different settings for BBC adventure series. Some of these are real places, while others are entirely fictional. Delete one letter from each pair to reveal all eight places, and then match each location with the series it features in from the right-hand column. For bonus points, three of these adventure series were broadcast on Radio 4. Which three?

1. AC VA LM EO NL ON TE	*ElvenQuest*
2. VD UI LS CS WA ON RU LS SD	*Eric*
3. HL IO DWD LE RE EW OA RL TD HS	*His Dark Materials*
4. AN TO RL TA HN UT MA BS RI IA AS	*Merlin*
5. FO AT NH TE AR WS OI RA LS DK	*Pilgrim*
6. NO RX FO OL RK DS	*The Railway Children*
7. NS OT UT TH HS WE SA TL ER OS	*Wizards vs Aliens*
8. SY CO TR KL SA HN DI SR RE	*Wolfblood*

LEGENDARY FIGURES

Six principal characters from the adventure series *Merlin* are listed here, with every second letter removed. Can you restore the missing letters to identify them all? Each of these characters appear in the original Arthurian legends, except for one. Which one?

G_I_S

_O_G_N_

G_I_E_E_E

_E_L_N

U_H_R

_R_H_R

THE CHRONICLES OF NARNIA

Before entire universes could be rendered via the state-of-the-art visual effects that were employed in creating the popular blockbuster film series, the BBC produced a much-loved adaptation of C.S. Lewis' fantasy novels. An international success, the series saw adaptations of the first four novels from the author and Oxbridge academic's seven-part series.

Lewis published his novels between 1950 and 1956. The novels detail the adventures of the Pevensie children, alongside characters associated with them, as they journey into the fantastical worlds of Narnia. The series was first adapted by the BBC in the 1980s for a 15-hour audio adaptation that was aired on Radio 4. On 13 November 1988, a three-series, 18-part adaptation began airing. The adaptation of the first book was directed by Marilyn Fox, while adaptations of the second and third books, which made up the second series, and the fourth book, were directed by Alex Kirby.

In 1984, the BBC scored a huge success with their adaptation of John Mansfield's 1953 children's fantasy *The Box of Delights*. A big-budget – for the time – wildly imaginatve, six-part series that employed extensive and groundbreaking visual and special effects, it set a high, award-winning standard for fantasy drama. *The Chronicles of Narnia* went further in creating an admired adaptation that captured the magic and majesty of Lewis' fiction, and proved hugely successful around the world.

Scenes from *The Chronicles*: (left) the Pevensie children with Aslan the talking lion; (right) Barbara Kellerman as the White Witch.

THE CHRONICLES OF NARNIA

Disguised below are the names of all seven books in the *Chronicles of Narnia* series, although one letter has been changed in each word to disguise them. Can you restore the book titles?

1. **TOE LOON, TIE WATCH ANY SHE BARDROBE**

2. **PRANCE CASTIAN**

3. **TIE BOYAGE IF SHE DOWN TREATER**

4. **THY SOLVER CHAIN**

5. **TOE WORSE ANT HAS TOY**

6. **TEE MALICIAN'S NESHEW**

7. **SHE LOST CATTLE**

CIRCULAR TALES

Can you work out how to rotate the rings below so that all of the solutions to the following questions can be read simultaneously, reading outwards from the centre of the circle?

1. **What is the name of the oldest Pevensie child?**
2. **Which Pevensie child is given a bow and arrow by Father Christmas, which is said to never miss its target?**
3. **What is the name given to the benevolent lion in *The Chronicles of Narnia*?**
4. **What type of woman lives in Cair Paravel at the beginning of the first story?**
5. **On what kind of stone structure is the lion sacrificed in the first story?**
6. **What is the surname of the professor with whom the Pevensie children are sent to stay during the war – and through whose wardrobe they travel to magical lands?**

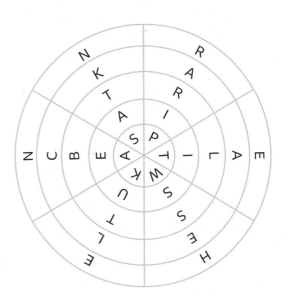

SPIES AND SPOOKS

For many, there's nothing quite so alluring as the spy genre. The intrigue entices, while the promise of exotic locations can be an irresistible draw. However, not all spy thrillers revel in glamorous worlds.

Recent series such as *Spooks*, *Hunted*, *The Night Manager* and *Killing Eve* embraced the thrill of action and location, while doing much to challenge genre conventions. There are also examples of pre-Cold War espionage dramas, such as the BBC's 1952 adaptation of John Buchan's *The Three Hostages*, featuring the heroic Richard Hannay, best known for his debut appearance in the author's 1915 thriller *The Thirty-Nine Steps*. More recently, *Spies of Warsaw* (2013) looked at the world of espionage in Poland prior to the outbreak of the Second World War.

But it is in the silent conflict between the capitalist West and communist East that the spy genre really took off. If *Act of Betrayal* (1971) focused on the lesser-known Portland Affair of the late 1950s, the Cambridge Spy ring inspired a variety of dramas, from the more factually oriented *Cambridge Spies* (2003) and Alan Bennett's *An Englishman Abroad* (1983) and *A Question of Attribution* (1991) to the BBC's celebrated John le Carré's trilogy adaptations *Tinker Tailor Soldier Spy* (1979), *Smiley's People* (1982) and *A Perfect Spy* (1987). More recently, a fictional counterpart to le Carré's George Smiley can be found in Johnny Worricker, an MI5 official caught up in the dirty politics of a post-9/11 world, in David Hare's *Page 8* (2008), *Turks and Caicos* (2014) and *Salting the Battlefield* (2014).

Matthew Macfadyen and Keeley Hawes in the roles of Tom Quinn and Zoe Reynolds in *Spooks*, a show that ran for ten series between 2002 and 2012.

FOLLOWING VILLANELLE

In the spy drama *Killing Eve*, the titular Eve follows the assassin Villanelle across Europe as she tries to uncover her secret identity. Hidden in the list to the right are the names of nine cities that Villanelle visits, although they have all been encrypted in a particular way. Can you break the encryption and therefore work out where Villanelle has been?

VLPBMARBA

IOAEOMOAB

ENRRSSMRE

NDILCTECR

NOSIOEED

ANNWRLE

DOE

ANN

MA

CHAIN REACTION

Can you find an intelligence operative hiding in each of the pyramids below? Solve each of the clues to reveal a word, with one letter per gap. Each successive word uses exactly the same letters as the previous solution, plus an extra one – although not necessarily in the same order.

1.

_ _ _	See
_ _ _ _	Nimble
_ _ _ _ _ (on)	Hunts
_ _ _ _ _ _	Compensates
_ _ _ _ _ _ _	Competitors
_ _ _ _ _ _ _ _	In small numbers

2.

_ _ _	'Perfect' number?
_ _ _ _	Spotless
_ _ _ _ _	Broker
_ _ _ _ _ _	Attractor
_ _ _ _ _ _ _	Item of clothing
_ _ _ _ _ _ _ _	Polemic

3.

_ _ _	Type of tree
_ _ _ _	Skin blemish
_ _ _ _ _	Roadside inn
_ _ _ _ _ _	Aggressively harass
_ _ _ _ _ _ _	Marks with blotches
_ _ _ _ _ _ _ _	Furthest from the right

4.

_ _ _	Took a seat
_ _ _ _	Compass point
_ _ _ _ _	Resource
_ _ _ _ _ _	United territories?
_ _ _ _ _ _ _	Corroborates
_ _ _ _ _ _ _ _	Most shrewd

TINKER TAILOR SOLDIER SPY

Like the elusive ring sought by Saruman in J.R.R. Tolkien's epic, when it comes to espionage on television, there is one series – and a defining character of the British spy establishment – to rule them all. The 1979 adaptation of John le Carré's acclaimed novel revelled in narrative complexity and moral ambiguity, and was dominated by an extraordinary tour-de-force performance by Alec Guinness as the sublime George Smiley.

Smiley's career in the British Secret Intelligence Service appears to have reached an end following the botched Operation Testify in Czechoslovakia. A mission to uncover a mole high up in the Circus, the group at the very heart of British intelligence, results in the capture and torture of British spy Jim Prideaux. Smiley is ousted along with Control, the head of the service. At least, to all concerned, he is. But Smiley is actually carrying out his own covert mission, into the very heart of the Circus, to uncover which of the four remaining men is the Soviet agent.

Like his previous *The Spy Who Came in from the Cold*, le Carré's 1974 novel brought the dour, grey reality of the espionage business to light. This wasn't so much a different environment to Ian Fleming's Bond series as an entire world away. There were no exotic locations or thrilling moments of action; just the pen-pushing antics of bureaucrats playing power games. But it was no less thrilling. The series remained faithful to the complexity and mundanity of le Carré's vision. But it was powered by a superb cast and Guinness' nuanced lead turn. He would return in the BBC's 1982 adaptation of *Smiley's People*.

Cast members from the 1979 adaptation of the story: (above) Hywel Bennett as field agent Ricki Tarr with Susan Kodicek as Irina; (right) Alec Guinness as Smiley.

LAST MAN STANDING

Hidden in the grid below are 13 of the 14 listed characters from *Tinker Tailor Soldier Spy*. The 14th has deserted the rest, however, and cannot be found in the grid – and is in fact the name of the Soviet mole who is uncovered in the series. Who is that double agent?

ALLELINE
BLAND
CONTROL
ESTERHASE
GUILLAM
HAYDON
IRINA
KARLA
LACON
MENDEL
PRIDEAUX
SACHS
SMILEY
TARR

U	R	O	K	J	T	D	M	T	T	R
E	S	T	E	R	H	A	S	E	I	E
P	N	X	U	C	L	M	A	Q	R	N
R	L	M	X	L	I	M	C	K	I	N
I	U	L	I	L	J	F	H	N	N	O
D	D	U	E	L	R	E	S	M	A	C
E	G	Y	X	D	P	L	E	J	A	A
A	F	L	O	R	T	N	O	C	L	L
U	B	L	A	N	D	T	A	R	R	M
X	S	H	W	E	P	O	M	W	A	S
K	A	L	L	E	L	I	N	E	K	Z

THE SPY RING

Five different synonyms for 'spy' have been hidden in the ring below. By rearranging the letters, can you find them all? Each letter is used for only one of the words, and there are no unused letters.

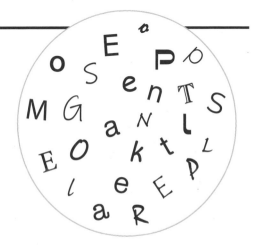

SCIENCE FICTION

British television sci-fi series may lack the scale of their US counterparts, but they have made up for this with clever storytelling . . . and the creation of one of the genre's best-loved and most memorable figures.

Doctor Who has become such a significant part of popular sci-fi culture that the character is as well-known around the world as *Star Trek*'s James T. Kirk. First appearing on BBC One in 1963, the Doctor has been a mainstay of British television – with the occasional break – for six decades. The series has also spawned off-shoots of varying success. If 1981's planned series *K-9 and Company* didn't get past its first episode, *Torchwood* and *The Sarah Jane Adventures* proved more enduring.

Nigel Kneale was a pivotal figure in sci-fi at the BBC. He created *The Quatermass Experiment*, which aired in 1953 and spawned subsequent films and series. Kneale also wrote an adaptation of George Orwell's *Nineteen Eighty-Four* (1954), *The Year of the Sex Olympics* (1968) – a dystopian drama that some have seen as presaging the arrival of reality television – and the television play, *The Stone Tape* (1972).

Popular sci-fi series continued, including the unsettling *Doomwatch*, *The Changes* and *Survivors*, the enjoyably cheesy *Blake's 7*, a faithful adaptation of John Wyndham's *The Day of the Triffids*. Children enjoyed the alien series *Tripods* while Russell T. Davies, who breathed new life into *Doctor Who*, created *Dark Season*, featuring a young Kate Winslet, and *Century Falls*. And for those who preferred their sci-fi in a more satirical tone, Douglas Adams adapted his acclaimed 1978 radio series *The Hitchhiker's Guide to the Galaxy* into a popular 1981 series, while *Red Dwarf* began its journey into deep space in 1988.

The cast of *Blake's 7*, with Gareth Thomas (centre front) in the lead role. The show ran for four series from 1978–81.

THE BBC'S GUIDE TO THE GALAXY

This may appear to be a list of 13 BBC programmes, but it actually conceals a series of directions to travel around the letter-based galaxy shown below. Can you uncover the hidden movement instructions and then apply them to the galaxy, beginning at the arrow and moving to one planet per programme? This means that you will visit 13 letter planets in all. The phrase spelled out as you visit the planets is also used to describe Earth in *The Hitchhiker's Guide to the Galaxy*. What is it?

1. **Coupling**
2. **My Left Nut**
3. **Love Soup**
4. **Puppy Love**
5. **Pinwright's Progress**
6. **The Wright Way**
7. **Down to Earth**
8. **The Kids Are All Right**
9. **RuPaul's Drag Race UK**
10. **Upstart Crow**
11. **Wright Around the World**
12. **Two Doors Down**
13. **Watership Down**

S A I Z R R M

M X E N Y L E

T K L Y H M S

J N T Y A R S

T E S O R B G

R S A M Y O T

RADIO DRAMA

Eight short stories by H.G. Wells, all of which have been dramatized and broadcast on BBC Radio 4, are each listed twice below. In the left-hand column, each story title has been rephrased, while in the right-hand column the original title is given but all the letters found in 'H.G. Wells' have been removed. The two lists are not in the same order. Can you identify the original titles?

The Precious Objects in the Large Wood
In the Deep Chasm
The Battle of the Planets
The Portal in the Brick-built Barrier
The Earliest Males in Earth's Closest Satellite
The Novel Device to Increase Speed
The Ocean Looters
A Reverie of Apocalypse

A Dram of Armaddon
In t Aby
T a Raidr
T ar of t ord
T Door in t a
T Firt Mn in t Moon
T N Accrator
T Traur in t Fort

DOCTOR WHO

The longest-running science-fiction television series centres on an extra-terrestrial time-traveller capable of regeneration. The series takes us into the past and future, journeys through galaxies and across countless planets. But through it all, the Doctor not only appears to prefer humanity above all other species, they have a singular and timeless fascination with the notion of Britishness.

The Doctor was from the planet Gallifrey, the home to the Time Lords, and travelled the universe in a TARDIS (Time and Relative Dimension in Space), a vehicle that resembled a 1960s London police box that was larger on the inside than it appeared on the outside. He battled a variety of alien (and human) aggressors, most notably the Daleks, who first appeared in the series' second episode, along with the Cybermen and a rogue Time Lord known as the Master.

The series was first created in 1963 by Sydney Newman, Donald Wilson and C.E. Webber, along with producer Verity Lambert, then the BBC's only female drama producer, as well as the youngest. Its first episode aired on 23 November 1963 and featured William Hartnell in the title role. After four series he was replaced by Patrick Troughton, then ten other male Doctors until Jodie Whittaker was cast as the first female Doctor in 2018. A constant among all Doctors is that each is accompanied on their various adventures by a human companion.

The initial run of Doctors was from 1963 to 1989, when the series was cancelled due to declining popularity. An unsuccessful attempt to revive the show was made in 1996, before it was successfully regenerated, with Russell T. Davies at the helm, in 2005. Like the series' protagonist, the theme music, created by the innovative BBC Radiophonic Workshop, has undergone a number of mutations, but at its core remains the same piece that first introduced the Doctor to our world.

The Daleks – among the most recognizable of Doctor Who's enemies – have been mimicked nationwide, for their shrill cry of 'exterminate, exterminate'.

HIDDEN VILLAIN

Listed below are the names of nine of Doctor Who's adversaries, but there is a further villain hiding in the grid. Who is it?

Place each of the given entries into the grid, one per row and with one letter per box (reading left to right), so that the name of the tenth foe is revealed by reading down the shaded column. Spaces between words have been omitted.

AUTONS
CYBERMEN
DAVROS
SLITHEEN
THE MASTER
THE SILENCE
TOCLAFANE
WEEPING ANGELS
ZYGONS

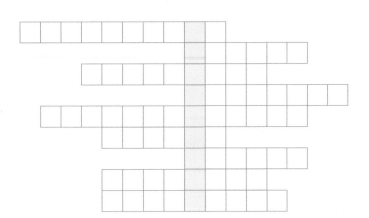

RESTORING ORDER

Shown on this page are the first 13 Doctors, in no particular order. When the images are rearranged in chronological order of appearance, the clue letters in the bottom left-hand corner of each photo can be read off in order to spell out the name of one of the Doctor's companions.

Can you work out the order in which the doctors appeared, and therefore reveal which assistant has had their name jumbled across time and space? The image with no letter indicates a space between the companion's two names.

RADIOPHONIC WORKSHOP

With the increasing sophistication of radio in the 1950s, a team was set up to generate 'radiophonic' sounds and effects for programmes. It would be responsible for one of the most famous television theme songs.

The workshop was created in 1958, in order to generate incidental sounds and audio effects, for radio and, later, television, that could match what was being created visually. Through the encouragement of pioneering producers such as Desmond Briscoe, Daphne Oram, Donald McWhinnie and Frederick Bradnum, the BBC Radiophonic Workshop was set up. It comprised a variety of individuals who mostly worked in composition or studio production. Among them was Delia Derbyshire, whose various accomplishments became the subject of the documentary *Delia Derbyshire: The Myths and Legendary Tapes* (2020).

The team, whose members regularly changed, operated out of Room 13 at Maida Vale studios, in London. Over the years they provided the theme and incidental music, as well as effects, for many BBC productions, including later episodes of *Quatermass and the Pit* (1958), *The Goon Show* (1951–60), *Penda's Fen* (1974), *Blake's 7* (1978–81), *The Hitchhiker's Guide to the Galaxy* (1981) and *The Living Planet* (1984). But their most famous creation was the shimmering theme music to *Doctor Who*, along with many of the series' otherworldly effects. The workshop was eventually closed in 1998, but its influence has been great – not just over sound effects for broadcast, but in the development of electronic music generally.

Delia Derbyshire came up with the arrangement for the *Doctor Who* theme tune. Here, she is pictured with Desmond Briscoe.

CUT THE TAPE

As well as the iconic theme tune, the BBC Radiophonic Workshop created several pieces of incidental music for *Doctor Who* episodes. The names given to ten of these tracks have been unfortunately cut apart below – much like the tapes used in the workshop to create them.

Reunite the first part of each track (left) with its second half (right) by drawing a straight line to join their dots. When paired up correctly, the matching lines pass through the letters of a cutting-edge device used in the workshop. Read from top to bottom to reveal its name.

Four • — • in Space
Planet • — • of Androzani
Revenge • — • of Decay
State • — • of Fire
Terror • — • of the Cybermen
The Caves • — • of the Deep
The Keeper • — • of the Rani
The Mark • — • of the Vervoids
The Wheel • — • of Traken
Warriors • — • to Doomsday

WORDS AND WAVES

Cutting, splicing and overlaying sounds formed much of the work of the Radiophonic Workshop. The technique of using non-instrumental (or 'found') sounds allowed creators to create music using both non-traditional methods and, often, non-traditional instruments.

In the image below, six objects used to create sounds for the workshop have each been written on their own 'wave', and then all six have been superimposed on top of one another to create an unusual soundscape. Can you identify all six objects that were used?

BBC FILM

Although the BBC has long been involved in filmmaking, the creation of a standalone production company is a relatively recent move in the corporation's history. Since its inception, BBC Film has been responsible for a long line of award-winning and box-office successes, both by British and international filmmakers.

BBC Film (originally known as BBC Films) was founded in 1990 by David M. Thompson, then a film programmer and documentary director. Though wholly owned by the BBC, it operated independently, with offices in central London. Thompson left in 2007 when BBC Film was more fully integrated into the organization, coming under the umbrella of BBC Vision. It changed its name in 2020, but its style of operation has remained consistent since its inception, producing an average of eight films a year.

The first major hit BBC Film had was in a co-production with independent film company Working Title on Stephen Daldry's *Billy Elliot* (2000), followed by Curtis Hanson's *Wonder Boys* (2000). It has worked with a variety of British filmmakers and their films, including Michael Winterbottom, with *Code 46* (2003) and *A Cock and Bull Story* (2005), Richard Eyre, with *Iris* (2001) and *Notes on a Scandal* (2006), Amma Asante, with *A United Kingdom* (2016), Gurinder Chadha's *Viceroy's House* (2017), Harry Macqueen's *Supernova* (2020) and Kevin MacDonald's *The Mauritanian* (2021). It has also worked with international directors, on projects such as David Cronenberg's *Eastern Promises* (2007), Gillian Armstrong's *Death Defying Acts* (2007), Thomas Vinterberg's *Far From the Madding Crowd* (2015) and Eliza Hittman's *Never Rarely Sometimes Always* (2020).

Jamie Bell in the lead role of Stephen Daldry's *Billy Elliot*, a story about gender, class and dancing set in the northeast of England during the 1980s.

ADAPTED ADAPTATIONS

Several films created by BBC Film are adaptations of well-known books. Eight of them have been disguised below, by changing exactly one letter in each word of the film/book's title. Can you identify all of the adapted works, and their authors (whose initials are given)?

1. **A RAPTURE TIE CATTLE** by D S
2. **BRIGHTEN RUCK** by G G
3. **FAN FROG SHE PADDING CROWN** by T H
4. **I SONG WAS DAWN** by N H
5. **LANE TYRE** by C B
6. **SHE LAZY ON TOE MAN** by A B
7. **TEE DEN WHY STORE IT GNATS** by J R
8. **TOE LOWER IF SHE DUG** by T S

THE LINE-UP

Each clue on the left can be solved to reveal the one-word title of a film from BBC Film. To help you reveal the names, their synopses are given on the right, although the two lists are not in the same order. Once you have revealed all the titles, sort them into alphabetical order. What do you 'initially' notice about the new line-up?

1. **Type of swimming race** (9)
2. **New York City borough/ bridge** (8)
3. **Having a characteristic rise and fall, as an accent** (7)
4. **Coloured part of the eye** (4)
5. **5th-century BC Roman general** (10)
6. **Insubordination, e.g.** (12)
7. **Respire** (7)

- A group of women seek to interrupt the 1970 Miss World competition, starring Keira Knightley
- A mother grieves for her son alongside his lover, though they have no common language, starring Ben Whishaw
- A young Irish woman struggles to adapt to life on both sides of the Atlantic, starring Saoirse Ronan
- A young man paralyzed by polio rebuilds his life with the help of his wife, starring Claire Foy and Andrew Garfield
- Adaptation of one of Shakespeare's tragedies, starring Ralph Fiennes
- Two would-be students fall in love over basketball lessons, despite external efforts to keep them apart, starring Arinzé Kene
- The real-life story of a writer with Alzheimer's and her husband, starring Judi Dench and Jim Broadbent

Comedy

Much-admired comedy writer Barry Cryer, whose work on BBC radio and television spanned decades, once noted, 'Analysing comedy is like dissecting a frog. Nobody laughs and the frog dies.' Accepting that comedy works is enough for some, but finding that elusive formula to repeated success is a grail that many writers, producers and performers have painstakingly sought. Radio comedy originally emerged out of variety shows, but in the 1950s, with the growing popularity of the sitcom, it developed into its own, multi-faceted platform. *Hancock's Half Hour* started in radio before moving to television, by which time comedy shows were increasing in numbers and styles. If Tony Hancock gave us a variation on everyday life – as later comedies, from *Fawlty Towers* to *Fleabag* would – *The Goon Show* revelled in the madcap, offering a surreal and frequently ridiculous perspective on the world. The show inspired *Monty Python*, *The Goodies* and *Shooting Stars*. Meanwhile, the absurdity of political life and shifts in societal attitudes informed everything from *That Was the Week That Was* and *Yes, Minister* to *The Young Ones* and *The Thick of It*.

CLASSIC COMEDY

When it comes to classic comedy, the most beloved of comedy entertainers are arguably Eric Morecambe and Ernie Wise. *The Morecambe and Wise Show* first aired on BBC Two – the only channel then broadcasting in colour – in 1968. Their routine combined sketches with variety show song-and-dance elements, all of which played to their odd-couple routine. In the 1970s, their Christmas specials often attracted the largest of any show throughout the year.

The Two Ronnies (1971–87) also set a high watermark in sketch-based comedy. Over the years, they were joined by Lenny Henry, Tracey Ullman and David Copperfield in *Three of a Kind*, as well as double acts featuring Mel Smith and Griff Rhys Jones, Dawn French and Jennifer Saunders, Stephen Fry and Hugh Laurie and other classic comedy sketch shows such as *The Mary Whitehouse Experience*, *The Fast Show* and, more recently, *Famalam*.

If Eric and Ernie drew on a classic tradition of British comedy, other shows went further afield. The Goons scored a huge success with their radio show and would prove to be a huge inspiration for the *Monty Python's Flying Circus* team. They were followed by another popular, off-the wall act in *The Goodies* (1970–82), featuring Tim Brooke-Taylor, Graeme Garden and Bill Oddie, whose humour was arguably more family-friendly than *Monty Python*'s. It's possible to see this lineage in off-the-wall comedy continuing with *Little Britain*, while the pairing of Vic Reeves and Bob Mortimer in the show *The Smell of Reeves and Mortimer* balanced surreal humour with a style that owed much to Morecambe and Wise.

The Two Ronnies (above left) were masters of clever script-writing.
Personality played a huge role in the humour of Morecambe and Wise (right).

ON THE DOUBLE

Draw straight lines to pair up these iconic comedy duos, joining the dots next to their surnames. When complete, the lines will pass through certain letters that will spell out, from top to bottom, the name of a famous comedy troupe. Each pair uses one surname from each column.

Armstrong
Baddiel
Barker
French
Fry
Giedroyc
Mayall
Mitchell
Morecambe
Reeves
Smith

Corbett
Edmondson
Laurie
Miller
Mortimer
Perkins
Rhys Jones
Saunders
Skinner
Webb
Wise

FIRST NAME BASIS

Once you have reunited the surnames in the puzzle above, can you identify which duo each of these first-name pairs belongs to?

- **Alexander and Ben**
- **David and Frank**
- **David and Robert**
- **Dawn and Jennifer**
- **Eric and Ernie**
- **Mel and Griff**

- **Mel and Sue**
- **Rik and Ade**
- **Ronnie and Ronnie**
- **Stephen and Hugh**
- **Vic and Bob**

DAD'S ARMY

A comedy about a group of British Home Guard volunteers during the Second World War was an unlikely hit that ran for nine years and 80 episodes. It also resulted in a feature spin-off, a radio series and a stage show, and has become one of the BBC's most beloved sitcoms.

The idea for the show was conceived by Jimmy Perry, who had been a member of the Local Defence Volunteers (later named the Home Guard) during the war. He was appearing in a sitcom written by David Croft. He showed him an episode and Croft passed it on to producer Michael Mills at the BBC, who commissioned a series. Mills changed the name from *The Fighting Tigers* to *Dad's Army* and the location from Brightsea-on-Sea to Walmington-on-Sea.

Arthur Lowe played the stentorian but slightly inept Captain Mainwaring, with John Le Mesurier as his second-in-command Sergeant Arthur Wilson. Clive Dunn was one of the cast's younger members, but played the ageing Lance Corporal Jack Jones. The rest of the troop comprised John Laurie as Private James Frazer – a Scot introduced to the series at the request of Michael Mills – James Beck as black market spiv Private Joe Walker, Arnold Ridley as the sensitive Private Charles Godfrey and Ian Lavender as relative youngster Private Frank Pike.

The show revelled in playing with British stereotypes and attitudes, most notably one of the most popular episodes, involving the capture of a German U-Boat crew. For most of its original run, the series attracted viewing figures approaching 20 million, a testament to a series that Perry and Croft initially felt had limited appeal.

Captain Mainwaring and his men found themselves in all manner of hilarious madcap capers.

UNDER FIRE

Below are six English expressions that relate in some way to combat or warfare. Every word in each expression, however, has had exactly one letter changed. Can you reveal all six original expressions? For example, 'UDDER WIRE' could be changed to 'UNDER FIRE'.

1. **BILE TOE BALLET**
2. **LAST SHE CATTLE PUT SON TEE WAD**
3. **LOUSE CANYON**
4. **MIGHT FINE WITS DIRE**
5. **TALE TIE FLAT**
6. **YOB ANY THOSE ARMS**

THE LINE-UP

Can you name each of the *Dad's Army* characters in this image? They are all described in the text opposite. Write each character's surname in the relevant space below, looking at the image from left (surname 1) to right (surname 6). For surname 7, write the name of the only character mentioned opposite *not* to appear in the photo.

Then, use the 'coordinates' after each name to reveal whether your troops have been correctly assembled. The first 'coordinate' is the position of a letter in the character's surname, and the second 'coordinate' is the position in which you should place that letter to reveal the hidden phrase below.

1: _____ (3, 5)

2: _____ (2, 3)

3: _____ (3, 1)

4: _____ (4, 6)

5: _____ (2, 4)

6: _____ (6, 2)

7: _____ (6, 7)

PHRASE: ＿＿ ＿＿＿＿＿＿

SITCOMS

The world's first, regular, half-hour, televised sitcom was *Pinwright's Progress*, written by Rodney Hobson and aired on the BBC from 1946–47. But it was Tony Hancock's collaboration with Ray Galton and Alan Simpson on *Hancock's Half Hour* that really cemented the popularity of the form. It was joined by the school-set *Whack-O!* and popular military comedy *The Army Game*. As much a barometer of the times as the soap opera, the sitcom often reflected attitudes regarding class, race, gender and morality.

The 1960s saw the sitcom increase in popularity, with shows like *Marriage Lines*, *The Rag Trade*, Galton and Simpson's *Steptoe and Son*, *The Likely Lads* and *The Liver Birds*, which was written by Carla Lane, who would go on to create *Butterflies*, *Solo* and *Bread*. Three other

key writers of the period were Jimmy Perry, David Croft and Jeremy Lloyd. Between them, they created *Dad's Army, Are You Being Served?, It Ain't Half Hot Mum, Hi-de-Hi!* and *'Allo 'Allo!*

The domestic set-up was lampooned in a variety of shows, from the more conventional *The Good Life*, *Terry and June*, *To the Manor Born*, *Birds of a Feather*, *Keeping Up Appearances* and *One Foot in the Grave* to the surreal *The Rise and Fall of Reggie Perrin*, the slyly satirical *The Royale Family* and beloved *Only Fools and Horses* and *Last of the Summer Wine*. *Porridge* took the form into the prison, *The Young Ones* offered a contemporary take on domestic life, *Absolutely Fabulous* added glamour, and both *Up Pompeii!* and *Blackadder* took the sitcom into the past. In the meantime, *Fawlty Towers* and *The Office* pushed comedy to the extreme, creating a world that was as excruciating as it was hilarious.

Scenes from two all-time favourite BBC sitcoms, *The Good Life* (above) and *Only Fools and Horses* (top right).

BLACKADDER THROUGH THE AGES

Each of *Blackadder*'s four series took place in a different historical era, from the Middle Ages through to the First World War, with each series set in a more recent era than the last. Can you match each of these images with one of the series titles below?

- **Series 1: *The Black Adder***
- **Series 2: *Blackadder II***
- **Series 3: *Blackadder the Third***
- **Series 4: *Blackadder Goes Forth***

FABULOUSLY ABSOLUTE

Place one of A, E, H, J, L, N, O, S and T into each empty square, so that no letter repeats in any row, column or bold-lined 3×3 box. Once the puzzle is solved, a name can be read across the shaded squares, belonging to a well-known artist who appeared in the final series of *Absolutely Fabulous.*

	J	H				N	S	
S			N		E			H
A								O
	T			A			J	
			E		T			
	E			S			N	
L								J
J			S		N			T
	H	E				S	L	

FAWLTY TOWERS

Few comedy shows have remained as popular as this series, which unfolds in a ramshackle British seaside hotel. A sharp and consistently funny skewering of attitudes towards class, gender, race, social mores and the notion of Britishness, the show revolves around a small ensemble of characters who work at the hotel or are permanent guests, alongside a small group of visitors new to each episode.

Created by John Cleese and Connie Booth, the two star as Basil Fawlty, the co-owner of the hotel with his wife Sybil (Prunella Scales), and Polly, the general assistant. There is also Andrew Sachs' heavily-accented Spanish waiter Manuel, Brian Hall's cockney chef Terry Hughes, Gilly Flower and Renee Roberts' dotty spinsters Miss Tibbs and Miss Gatsby, and Ballard Berkeley's amiable guest Major Gowen. All, wittingly or not, at some point find themselves the object of Basil's ire. He, in turn, is constantly under attack from Sybil for failing to keep the hotel in order.

The show only ran for two series of six episodes, but each was crafted into a finely tuned farce, often revolving around a single incident that soon spirals out of control. The impending visit of a health inspector, for instance, leads to a case of mistaken identity, a fire in the kitchen and, at the worst possible moment, the appearance of a rat. But, arguably, the most famous episode involves a group of German guests, Basil sustaining concussion and his tactless national stereotyping. The result is flawless comedy that has remained no less funny in the decades since it was first aired.

Playing the role of Basil Fawlty, John Cleese permanantly wore the angst-ridden face of a man on the edge of a nervous breakdown.

WORST FLAW YET

In the opening credits for each episode, the letters of the 'FAWLTY TOWERS' hotel sign have often been rearranged. Each of the 12 episode titles listed right has similarly had the letters of one of its words, marked in upper case, anagrammed. Can you untangle these jumbled words to reveal all of the original episode titles?

1. A COUTH of Class
2. The IDLERUBS
3. The DEWDING Party
4. The Hotel SCORNSPITE
5. TOURGEM Night
6. The ENGRAMS
7. COMICMOUNTAIN Problems
8. The SPIRITYACHTS
9. RAWFOLD Salad
10. The IRKPEP and the Corpse
11. The RAINYRAVENS
12. BAILS the Rat

QUITE QUOTABLE

Once you have revealed the names of the episodes in the previous puzzle, can you match each of the quotes below to the episode from which it comes? To help you, each line has been chosen so that it is relevant in some way to the title of the episode it appears in. All of the quotes belong to different episodes.

1. 'Don't mention the war.'

2. 'If you don't like duck . . . then you're rather stuck.'

3. 'I'll put an ad in the papers: "Wanted, kind home for enormous savage rodent. Answers to the name of Sybil."'

4. 'I'm so sorry, I'm afraid the dining room door seems to have disappeared.'

5. 'Now, please, please, try to understand before one of us dies.'

6. 'There's enough there for an entire convention.'

7. 'Oh, spiffing. Absolutely spiffing. Well done. Two dead, twenty-five to go.'

8. 'Yes, it's a traditional old English thing. It's apples, grapefruit and potatoes in a mayonnaise sauce.'

ALTERNATIVE COMEDY

In any art form, the 'new thing' is almost always regarded as alternative – a reaction to what came before. In the world of British comedy, this distinction was never more pronounced than in the appearance of a generation of writers, performers and stand-up comedians during Margaret Thatcher's first term as prime minister. Just as Thatcherism transformed British politics, culture and society, these alternative comedians challenged the status quo.

The new wave of comedy embraced the spirit of punk, challenging antiquated attitudes towards race, gender and sexuality. They ran the gamut, from the politically engaged to the absurd. But together they would transform the comedy environment. Many of them were graduates, but unlike the Oxbridge forbears that created *Beyond the Footlights*, *Monty Python* and *The Goodies*, they were from redbrick universities,

polytechnics and art and drama schools. A number of them made their debuts on the nascent comedy club scene that began with the creation of the Comedy Store in London, in 1980. In that same year, the BBC screened *Boom Boom . . . Out Go the Lights*, a showcase of talent that had emerged from the venue. It featured Alexei Sayle, Nigel Planer and Rik Mayall, who, with Adrian Edmondson and Christopher Ryan, would appear in *The Young Ones*, a seminal programme for this new generation. Alongside it was *A Kick Up the Eighties*, which also featured Mayall. He and Edmondson would later appear in *Filthy Rich & Catflap* and *Bottom*. But arguably the most successful members of this generation were the double acts of Stephen Fry and Hugh Laurie, and Dawn French and Jennifer Saunders, who would work together and individually over the course of the next few decades.

A scene from *The Young Ones* (above); Rik Mayall as the anorak-wearing reporter Kevin Turvey in *A Kick Up the Eighties* (right).

FRENCH AND SAUNDERS

Jumbled up below are the names of items that appeared on the *French and Saunders* sketch show. Much like the duo themselves, the items listed consist of two parts separated by the word 'and'. In this case, however, the various second parts of each title have become mixed up. Can you move each word or phrase after the 'and' back to the line it belongs to?

Six of the untangled pairs are the names of films, TV shows or bands that were parodied. The seventh is the name of a sketch.

1. **Beauty and Daughter**
2. **Modern Mother and Louise**
3. **Pride and the Beast**
4. **Rosemary and Prejudice**
5. **The Mamas and the Dead**
6. **The Quick and The Papas**
7. **Thelma and Thyme**

NO RELATION

One of the long-running jokes in *A Bit of Fry & Laurie* involved a speaker saying 'no relation' after mentioning the name of a new character – who indeed quite clearly had no relation to the speaker.

Each of the pairs of words listed right also have no relation. But if you change one letter in each capitalized word then you can create a common English expression where the two parts are related. For example, 'SO and FRY' could be changed to make 'TO and FRO'.

Can you identify all ten phrases?

1. **ALIKE and SELL**
2. **BARK and WORTH**
3. **BULLS and THISTLES**
4. **BUTS and BOYS**
5. **FINS and SANDY**
6. **THIN and WHAT**
7. **TRICK and FACT**
8. **AIM and RIGOUR**
9. **DARTS and ALE**
10. **WALL and GOLD**

MONTY PYTHON'S FLYING CIRCUS

The arrival of *Monty Python's Flying Circus* on the BBC signalled a landmark in television comedy. Anarchic, absurdist, taboo-breaking and bereft of any coherent structure, it delighted some, perplexed others, outraged more than a few and influenced subsequent generations of comedy writers and performers.

The show was conceived and performed by Graham Chapman, John Cleese, Eric Idle, Terry Gilliam, Terry Jones and Michael Palin. They were assembled by comedy writer Barry Took. All except Gilliam, who was responsible for the inventive and frequently outrageous animation on the show, came out of the Oxbridge Revue scene. They had previously been involved, both individually and collectively, in a variety of TV sketch and satirical shows when Cleese invited Palin to join him and Chapman on an idea for the BBC. Palin brought writing partner Jones and

Idle with him, with the latter suggesting Gilliam produce animation to accompany the sketches.

The first episode, 'Whither Canada', aired just before 11pm on Sunday 5 October 1969. It began with a signature cold opening – one of the show's many innovations – featuring Palin as a Robinson Crusoe character, struggling to emerge from the sea, who finally reaches the camera only to say 'It's…', before Gilliam's animation accompanies the theme music. From the outset, the series did away with conventional punchline gags. But after seeing Spike Milligan's *Q* (1969) series, which abandoned sketches abruptly, Jones encouraged the team to adopt a more stream-of-consciousness approach, with themes of jokes running across a whole episode. Over time, the impact of the series has been seismic. So much so that critics have equated *Monty Python* as being to comedy what The Beatles were to popular music.

The *Monty Python* team, from left to right: Terry Jones, Graham Chapman, John Cleese; Eric Idle, Terry Gilliam and Michael Palin.

UNEXPECTED ENDING

Each of these sketch titles has been given the wrong final word, highlighted in bold. Can you shuffle around the endings and restore the names of some of *Monty Python*'s most famous sketches?

1. Dead **Fork**
2. Dirty **Song**
3. Fish **Walks**
4. Marriage Guidance **World**
5. Seduced **Parrot**
6. The Funniest Joke in the **License**
7. The Lumberjack **Milkmen**
8. The Ministry of Silly **Inquisition**
9. The Spanish **Counsellor**

THE MAN WHO SPEAKS IN ANAGRAMS

In the sketch The Man Who Speaks in Anagrams, Eric Idle plays a man who is adapting the works of Shakespeare entirely into anagrams. Can you decipher the names of these Shakespeare plays, unjumbling each of the words in **bold**?

After revealing the bold words, place them once each into the grid, one letter per box. Once all the words are placed, the letters in the shaded squares can be rearranged to spell the full title of a further Shakespeare play. What is it?

- **Batchme**
- **Helltoo**
- **Inacolours**
- **Licebymen**
- Much Ado About **Onnight**
- **Resplice**
- **Rumease** for Measure
- The **Charmnet of Venice**
- The **Petsmet**
- The Two Gentlemen of **Raveno**
- The Winter's **Late**
- **Thelma**
- Timon of **Hasten**

FLEABAG

Funny, provocative and ultimately moving, Phoebe Waller-Bridge's screen adaptation of her one-woman stage show didn't so much capture the zeitgeist as steal it wholesale. From the audacity of episode one's prologue to its poignant final scene, *Fleabag* never puts a foot wrong – something that cannot quite be said of its refreshingly frank protagonist.

Expanding the canvass of her 2013 stage show, Waller-Bridge plays the eponymous twentysomething, exploring her sexuality, coping with grief, grappling with a fractious family and dealing with a tsunami of conflicting emotions as she goes about her everyday life in London.

She pursues a series of relationships – most notably Andrew Scott's 'sexy' Catholic priest – while coping with the loss of her friend and keeping the café she owns running. Her relationship with her father (Bill Patterson) is strained, due in no small part to the ambivalent relationship she has with the woman (Olivia Coleman) he intends to marry, an artist who has fine-tuned the art of passive aggression. And the sister (Sian Clifford) she was once close to is increasingly estranged, particularly after her brother-in-law (Brett Gelman) tries to hit on her.

From the outset, the show breaks the fourth wall, with Waller-Bridge's character addressing her desires and concerns directly to the audience, which makes the things she doesn't talk about all the more affecting. Integrating this mix of commentary and internal monologue seamlessly into the action, it allows the show to grapple with issues around femininity, sexuality, friendship and intimacy with no small insight and a depth that balances uproarious humour with moments of unrestrained emotion.

Phoebe Waller-Bridge in the title role. By the end of the first series, Fleabag's prospects for happiness are not riding high.

WHAT'S IN A NAME?

Scrambled below are the names of several characters from the show, all as officially named in the credits. Not all of the names are proper names, however – for example, one recurring character is simply credited as 'Bank Manager'.

Each name has also had one extra letter added, which, when extracted and read in turn, spell out the main characteristic of the character Hilary from the first series. Can you identify this characteristic, along with all of the characters?

1. **E.G. JAK**
2. **CUE LIAR**
3. **RAM IT IN**
4. **RH YARN**
5. **FABLE AGE**
6. **HOT, MAD OGRE**
7. **DP/DA**
8. **OIOB**
9. **STEEP RIGHT**

FIND THE STATUE

In the first series of the show, Fleabag steals – more than once – a small statue from her godmother, an artist whom she hates. Can you locate all the stolen statues that have been hidden in the grid opposite? Clues in some squares show the number of statues in touching squares – including diagonally. No more than one statue may be hidden per square, and no statues are in squares that contain numbers.

	2		2	1
	3		2	
1			2	
2				1
	2	2		1

THE OFFICE

An understated, low-key mockumentary, documenting life in a humdrum British office hardly seems the stuff of classic comedy. But Ricky Gervais and Stephen Merchant's creation has not only become one of the most widely admired comedies of the 2000s, it is also one of the most influential.

Unfolding over two six-episode series and a two-part Christmas special, *The Office* portrays life for a group of employees at a large paper company, Wernham Hogg (where 'life is stationary') based out of Slough Training Estate, in southeast England. Much of the action revolves around four main characters: Tim Canterbury, Gareth Keenan, Dawn Tinsley and their manager David Brent, played by Martin Freeman, Mackenzie Crook, Lucy Davis and Ricky Gervais. Much of the humour derives from

Brent attempting to ingratiate himself with his staff, Gareth's sycophancy towards his boss and the embarrassing situations they inadvertently place themselves in. In particular, Brent's conversations have no filter and often stray into NSFW territory, or show prejudices that are more the result of an idiotic thought than a desire to cause offence. Offset against this is the possibility of romance between Tim and Dawn, which resolves itself in the Christmas special.

Like *Fawlty Towers*, *The Office* profits from less is more, with Gervais and Merchant calling it a day after just two series and a special, save for a Comic Relief short *The Return of Brent* (2013) and the film *David Brent: Life on the Road* (2016). The US version of the show, which first aired in 2005 and starred Steve Carell, Rainn Wilson and John Krasinski, ran for nine seasons, ending in 2013.

David Brent hosts a staff meeting in his office – one of the many cringe-worthy scenes from the show.

MAKING CUTS

Eight episode titles from series 1 and 2 of *The Office* have been faced with cuts and redistribution below – that is, they have been cut into fragments, which have then been redistributed into alphabetical order. Can you reassemble them correctly to reveal all eight titles, each of which consists of a single word? Most of the episode titles could be considered 'office jargon'. In addition, a related ninth, decoy, word has been added, which is not an episode title, and is the only word to be split into four sections. What is it?

AN	APP	CY	DOW
ENT	ER	EW	GEM
INI	INTE	ION	IVAT
JUD	ME	MOT	NG
NSI	PA	RAI	RED
RG	RT	RVI	SALS
TRA	Y	UND	ZE

EMPLOYEE OF THE MONTH

The names of several characters in *The Office* feature below, along with their job titles. However, any letters in the word 'SLOUGH' have been removed. Can you fill in the gaps, to find out who does what?

DAVID BRENT: _ENERA_ MANA_ER

TIM CANTERB_RY: _A_E_ REPRE_ENTATIVE-

DAWN TIN__EY: C_MPANY RECEPTI_NI_T

RICKY __WARD: _FFICE TEMP

JENNIFER TAY__R-C_ARKE: _EAD _FFICE

D_NNA: W_RK EXPERIENCE

COMIC RELIEF

Along with *Children in Need*, which is broadcast on the BBC every November, Comic Relief's *Red Nose Day* is the UK's pre-eminent charity telethon, raising millions of pounds for causes around the world. Like Live Aid, Comic Relief was created in response to the startling images of widespread famine in Ethiopia, drawing on the talent pool of contemporary British comedy and popular culture to raise both money and awareness of urgent issues around the globe.

that could go towards helping an increasing variety of causes. The key event for the charity was *Red Nose Day*, an all-day event on the BBC dominated by sketches, comedy specials, stand-up, music performances, coverage of various charity events and reports from countries and organizations that will receive money. The first event was broadcast on 8 February 1988 and took place every two years.

In its first edition, the event raised £15 million. By 2015, Comic Relief, the *Red Nose Day* and the companion charity telethon *Sport Relief*, which was launched in conjunction with BBC Sport in 2002, had raised in excess of £1 billion for charity. In 2021, it was announced that *Red Nose Day* would become an annual event and, starting from 2022, there would be no more *Sport Relief* telethons.

Comic Relief was founded by popular comedian Lenny Henry and writer Richard Curtis. It was initially inspired by charity worker Jane Tewson, who established it as the operating name of Charity Projects, a registered charity in England and Scotland. The concept was simple – getting British audiences to laugh while reaching into their pockets for a donation

Lenny Henry and Davina McCall (above); David Walliams sports a red nose (right).

RED NOSE DAY

Below, eight shows and stories that have previously been turned into Comic Relief specials have been disguised by wearing red noses over one of their words. Can you work out which seven TV shows, and one classic children's story, they are?

1. **Beauty and the**

2.  **Who**

3. **of Duty**

4. **The** **of Dibley**

5. **University**

6. **'s Den**

7. **Little**

BARELY RECOGNIZABLE

The images below show two Comic Relief sketches that parodied a popular TV show and a well-known franchise, respectively. Can you work out the title of each sketch, based on the clues, and say what was being spoofed?

Affluent part of a city + ground floor in a two-storey house + monks' residence (6, 8, 5)

Arachnid + e.g. tree + adult male (6-5, 3)

POTTER PARODY

In 2003, the *Harry Potter* film franchise was parodied in a Comic Relief special, 'Harry Potter and the Secret Chamber Pot of Azerbaijan'. Listed below are four cast members who took part, although their names have been replaced with a description of their role in a different BBC show. Can you identify the four actors? The number of letters in their names is given.

1. **One Ronnie as Hagrid** (6, 7)
2. **The Vicar of Dibley as Harry Potter** (4, 6)
3. **Edina Monsoon as Ron Weasley** (8, 8)
4. **Gavin's Mum as Professor McGonagall** (6, 8)

Once you have identified the four actors, can you also work out which children's puppet with an alliterative name made an appearance as Dobby the House Elf? (5, 5)

89

RADIO COMEDY

Although it was immediately embraced across the Atlantic, comedy took some time to build its foundations on radio in the United Kingdom. The first significant success was *It's That Man Again*, featuring music-hall favourite Tommy Handley, which first aired in 1939. *Much-Binding-in-the-Marsh* followed in 1944. This also ran for a decade and starred Richard Murdoch and Kenneth Horne, the latter going on to further success with *Beyond Our Ken* and the hugely popular *Round the Horne*.

However, the two major breakthroughs for radio comedy in the United Kingdom were *The Goon Show* and *Hancock's Half Hour*. The former was an anarchic sketch series, mostly written by and starring Spike Milligan, alongside Peter Sellers, Michael Bentine and Harry Secombe, which ran from 1951–60. Its frequent edging towards the surreal proved influential not only for the later *Monty Python* team, but was also cited as an influence on The Beatles. *Hancock's Half Hour* began in 1954 and ran through six series, ending in 1959, while its television incarnation spanned 1956–61. It set the template for countless other radio series that made a successful transition to television, including *The Kenny Everett Show*, *Knowing Me, Knowing You with Alan Partridge*, *On the Town with The League of Gentlemen*, *Goodness Gracious Me*, *Mitchell and Webb*, *The Mighty Boosh* and *Little Britain*. Douglas Adams' *The Hitchhiker's Guide to the Galaxy* proved so popular that it spawned a series of novels along with a TV and big-screen adaptation.

If quiz shows such as *Whose Line Is It Anyway?* and *Have I Got News for You* successfully made their way to television, two other series remained long-standing favourites on radio only. Both *I'm Sorry I Haven't A Clue* and *Just a Minute* remain two of the most popular and longest-running shows on radio.

I'm Sorry I Haven't A Clue; from left to right: Graeme Garden, Tim Brooke-Taylor, pianist Colin Sell, Barry Cryer and chairman Humphrey Lyttelton.

LADIES OF LETTERS

Airing on Radio 4, *Ladies of Letters* revealed the lives of Irene and Vera through their correspondence across the course of 13 years. By reading the clues below, can you work out who is related to whom in each of their two families, matching each name to a numbered box on the family trees? Blue boxes depict male family members, and yellow boxes are female family members.

In the list of names, there are two '??'s – one each for the unknown husbands. Where multiple marriages are shown then the first, chronologically, is given on the left. Older siblings appear to the left of younger ones.

- Anthony is the partner of Vera's son Howard
- Brian's daughter is Bubbles
- Bubbles is Cheryl-Marie's younger half-sister
- Christopher is Irene's son, and has three children
- Howard has a daughter called Flo
- Karen and Lesley have both married twice, though neither of the first husbands' names are known
- Margaret is the mother of Little Christopher and his younger brother, Tommy
- Michaela is Irene's daughter-in-law, and the mother of Sophie-Irene
- Millie is Vera's granddaughter
- Nelson is Karen's son
- St John is Vera's son-in-law

Names to match:

??	Margaret
??	Michaela
Anthony	Millie
Brian	Nelson
Cheryl-Marie	St John
Christopher	Vera
Flo	Bubbles
Howard	Sophie-Irene
Irene	Little Christopher
Karen	Tommy
Lesley	

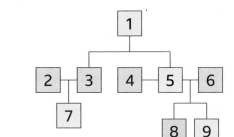

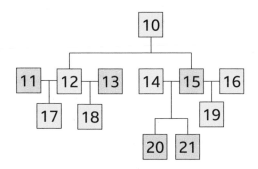

NEEDLE IN A HAYSTACK

Can you trace out the name of a popular Radio 4 comedy show in the grid opposite, by moving from square to square in any direction, including diagonally, one letter at a time? The name consists of two words, and each square is used once. The title of the show is also the name of the double act that performs on it.

P	E	H
I	N	T

THE HITCHHIKER'S GUIDE

Encompassing the beginning of the universe, its end and pretty much everything in between, Douglas Adams' singular, hilarious and consistently inventive sci-fi satire took aim at all manner of targets and successfully hit the bullseye each time. Taking the form of a novel, TV series, feature film, comic book, computer game and even a stage production, Adams' creation started out as a 1978 radio show.

The narrative revolves around Arthur Dent, a mild-mannered Englishman who encounters visiting alien Ford Prefect and is informed that Earth is about to be destroyed by a species of bureaucratic civil servants called the Vogons who are clearing a path in space for an intergalactic bypass. Escaping just before Earth explodes, Dent and Ford embark on a series of adventures, accompanied by two-headed Zaphod Beeblebrox, a depressed robot named Marvin and Trillian, the only other human survivor.

Adams came up with the story while writing a series called *The Ends of the Earth*, with each episode ending with the destruction of the planet. He added Ford Prefect, making him a researcher for a book that eventually became the series' title and the resulting show jettisoned everything from the original idea save for the destruction of Earth.

The radio adaptation proved so successful that Adams adapted it into a novel in 1979, followed by the sequels *The Restaurant at the End of the Universe* (1980), *Life, the Universe and Everything* (1982), *So Long, and Thanks for All the Fish* (1984) and *Mostly Harmless* (1992). The BBC produced a successful TV adaptation in 1981.

The sixth and final part of the radio series, called *The Hexagonal Phase*, aired in 2018 and starred many of the original cast members.

THE HITCHHIKER'S JOURNEY

Write a number into each empty square so that each number from 1 to 64 appears once in the grid. These numbers must form a path from 1 (yellow) to 64 (red), moving to a square one higher in value at each step as a king moves in chess: left, right, up, down or diagonally. Once complete, the green square will contain the number that is revealed to be the answer to the 'Ultimate Question of Life, the Universe and Everything'.

64					35		43
61		56	33				
	54	50	48			24	
52				29			
	1			27	26		21
	3	9	11		17		
4						16	

SPINNING AROUND

Can you work out how you could rotate the rings below so that all the answers to the following questions can be read simultaneously, reading outwards from the centre of the circle?

1. What is the surname of the actor who played Arthur Dent in the radio series?
2. What five-letter invented word is 'hitchhiker slang' for someone who is 'really amazingly together'?
3. Which household item is suggested throughout the franchise as being essential for any hitchhiker?
4. Which musical instrument featuring in the radio show's theme tune was chosen because it gave the music a sense of being on a road trip?
5. After the first radio series was produced, into what format did Adams next adapt his 'Hitchhiker' tales?
6. Which planet is blown up in the first episode of the radio series?

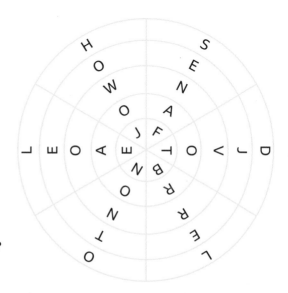

HANCOCK'S HALF HOUR

A show based around the trials and tribulations of co-creator, writer and lead character Tony Hancock, this radio and subsequent television series, which first aired in 1954 and ran for seven years, broke the mould for broadcast comedy. Shifting away from the variety format to a more situational style, the series was one of the earliest British examples of the sitcom.

Set in what was then East Cheam, in the southern part of Greater London, the show was devised by the writing team of Ray Galton and Alan Simpson with Hancock, who was already known to audiences through his appearances on the radio programmes *Educating Archie* (1950–60) and the variety show *Star Bill*. *Hancock's Half Hour* also featured a variety of revolving characters, played by Sid James,

Kenneth Williams, Bill Kerr, Moira Lister, Andrée Melly and Hattie Jacques.

Six series were recorded for radio, running from 1954–59. Seven were made for television, with significantly fewer episodes, airing between 1956 and 1961. Each show was similar in format, setting up a scenario and allowing the characters to interact around it. If earlier radio episodes were heavy on gags, as the series developed it gained a complexity in characterization, albeit with Hancock's grumpy protagonist (Anthony Aloysius St John Hancock) always at the centre, albeit in a variety of scenarios.

Hancock never repeated the runaway success of the show, whereas Galton and Simpson went on to score another success with *Steptoe and Son*. Nevertheless, some 40 years after the show's final episode aired on television, Hancock was voted the greatest British comedian of all time.

Tony Hancock (above) and showtime regular Sid James (right).

HANCOCK'S SECOND HALF

A number of episode titles from the radio series of *Hancock's Half Hour* are listed below. Can you fit all of the words marked in bold into the grid beneath, placing one letter per box, crossword-style?

1. The Americans Hit **Town**
2. The Blackboard **Jungle**
3. The Boxing **Champion**
4. The Chef That Died of **Shame**
5. The Christmas Eve **Party**
6. The Crown **Jewels**
7. The Department Store **Santa**
8. The Election **Candidate**
9. The End of the **Series**
10. The Espresso **Bar**
11. The First Night **Party**
12. The Foreign **Legion**
13. The Grappling **Game**
14. The Holiday **Camp**
15. The Income Tax **Demand**
16. The Insurance **Policy**
17. The Male **Suffragettes**

18. The Marrow **Contest**
19. The New **Car**
20. The Old School **Reunion**
21. The Pet **Dog**
22. The Prize **Money**
23. The Publicity **Photograph**
24. The Race **Horse**
25. The Sleepless **Night**
26. The Television **Set**
27. The Test **Match**
28. The Threatening **Letters**
29. The Three **Sons**
30. The Trial of Father **Christmas**
31. The Unexploded **Bomb**
32. The Wild Man of the **Woods**
33. The Winter **Holiday**

95

Soap Opera

From rural goings-on in Ambridge through to the hustle and bustle of Albert Square, the lives of characters on the long-running series *The Archers* and *EastEnders* have become an essential part of daily life for many audiences. These may be the most popular soaps on the BBC, but they are far from the only continual dramas to be produced over the course of the last 80 years. Some series have lasted one season, while others attracted interest for a period. But few have successfully navigated their way through generations, with characters akin to the members of viewers' extended families. The travails the characters experience have created countless water-cooler moments in the workplace. And the soaps that never quite enjoyed the longevity of their more successful counterparts nevertheless entertained while they lasted, whether it was crossing the North Sea by ferry or lapping up the sun on the Spanish coastline.

BBC SOAPS

Not all soap operas win the hearts of their audiences. For every *EastEnders*, *Coronation Street*, *Brookside* or *Hollyoaks*, there's the show that aimed high but only enjoyed a brief stint in the spotlight.

The BBC's first soap wasn't even targeted at a UK audience. *Front Line Family*, first broadcast in 1941, was a radio show aimed at US radio listeners to encourage them to support their troops' involvement in the Second World War. It was followed by *Mrs Dale's Diary* in 1948, which ran until 1969, and then *The Archers* in 1951.

The BBC's first adult televised soap was *The Grove Family*, which began airing in 1954 and remained a fixture on television until 1957. Like many subsequent soaps it was set in London and documented daily life for three generations of a family who were mostly employed in their building business. Aside from *EastEnders*, other

London-based soaps have included *199 Park Lane* (1965), set within a block of luxury flats and focusing on upper-middle-class lives, and *Compact* (1962–65), which unfolded in the offices of a magazine and featured the first regular Black character in a soap opera (Horace James). *The Brothers*, set within a haulage company, ran from 1972–76, while *Castles* only ran over the summer of 1995.

Further afield, there was *United* (1965–67), set within a fictional second-division football team, the luxury yachting soap *Howard's Way* (1985–90), and the highly successful and long-running Welsh-language soap *Pobol y Cwym* (1974), followed by Scotland's own *River City* in 2002. It's a contrast to what some see as the nadir of the British soap – a battle between the ferry drama *Triangle*, which ran between 1981 and 1983, and *El Dorado*, which ran for one year from July 1992 before being cancelled.

A scene from BBC Scotland's Glasgow-based *River City* (above); Kate O'Mara playing the role of Laura Wilde in *Howard's Way* (right).

SOAPS AND WATER

Each of these watery title cards from BBC soaps has had the name of its programme removed. All of the removed names can be found right, but with all the letters found in 'TV SOAP' removed. The body of water featured in each soap or its title card is given to help you. Can you restore the title to each opening credit shot? Note that one of the programmes is a Welsh-language show, with a Welsh title.

EENDER

ELDRD

HWRD' WY

RINGLE

RIER CIY

RWND RWND

River Thames

River Clyde

North Sea

Mediterranean Sea

English Channel

Irish Sea

COMPACT

Each of the following episode titles from the soap *Compact* is also a well-known idiom or expression. They have, however, all been made more 'compact' by having had their vowels removed. Can you restore the vowels and therefore reveal the original titles?

1. DWN TH HTCH
2. MMNT F TRTH
3. TH MN FR TH JB
4. CMNGS ND GNGS
5. RDNG FR FLL
6. LL THT JZZ
7. BSNSS S SL
8. SHCK TCTCS
9. SNT T CVNTRY
10. LV Y ND LV Y
11. TH TRTH WLL T

EASTENDERS

Created as a direct challenge to *Coronation Street*'s dominance over British television soap operas, *EastEnders* was an immediate hit with audiences. It has remained one of the BBC's most popular shows, in part through its desire to grapple with the social, political and cultural issues of contemporary Britain.

Twenty-three of the characters were created during a writing session in Lanzarote, with Holland drawing on his own family experiences to create the Beale and Fowler families. The first episode aired on 19 February 1985 and attracted an audience of 13 million.

Unfolding in Albert Square, in the fictional London borough of Walford, the series was originally intended to screen for 30 minutes, two evenings a week, with an omnibus episode airing on a Sunday afternoon. Since 2001, it has aired every weekday evening except Wednesdays. The cast was mostly composed of unknowns, with the exception of Wendy Richard, who had appeared in *Are You Being Served?* But for the show's huge audience, who tune in to every episode, each of these characters has become a very real part of their lives.

In the early 1980s, BBC executives were looking for a regular weekly soap. The producer/script editor team of Julia Smith and Tony Holland pitched the idea of a series that would run twice-weekly, every week of the year. It took another two years to develop, during which time they identified the East End of London as the perfect location for a close-knit community. By the time Smith and Holland had decided on the world they wanted to set their drama in, they had 11 months to write, cast and start shooting the series.

Barbara Windsor as Peggy Mitchell, landlady of the Queen Vic (above); Sharon Watts pictured with both of Peggy's sons, Phil and Grant (right).

FAMILIES ON THE SQUARE

Shown below are several iconic characters from *EastEnders*, along with their first names. Their surnames – which are the names of some of Walford's best-known families – can then be found in 'The Square' underneath. Find the names by tracing a path from letter to touching letter, in the same order as the characters below (left to right, top to bottom). Each letter is used exactly once, and the path starts at the star. If characters have had multiple surnames, it is up to you to find the correct one.

Ian

Martin

Max

Stacey

Peggy

Pat

Shabnam

Mick

Dot

Den

☆	A	L	E	F	R	B	R
B	E	C	T	O	E	N	A
L	E	H	I	W	L	N	I
L	T	C	M	R	E	T	N
B	U	H	E	R	C	A	G
M	R	E	T	T	O	L	S
A	O	D	R	T	W	A	S
S	O	C	A	O	N	T	T

CASUALTY

The longest-running medical drama in the world, *Casualty* has been saving lives on screen since it first aired on 6 September 1986. Set in the A&E department of a hospital in the west England city of Bristol, it has become one of the mainstays of Saturday night programming.

The series was created by Jeremy Brock and Paul Unwin. Their intention was to champion the National Health Service in the face of cuts by Margaret Thatcher's Conservative government. Moreover, they envisaged the series grappling with the major political, social and cultural issues of the day. The writers spent time in hospitals as part of their research and from there crafted a series in which a key event per episode was interspersed with continuing stories regarding the regular characters' lives,

all leavened with the humour that they found present even in the direst of circumstances.

The first series of *Casualty* introduced the regular members of the night shift, including nurses Megan Roach (Brenda Fricker), Clive King (George Harris), Lisa 'Duffy' Duffin (Cathy Shipton) and Charlie Fairhead (Derek Thompson), who, some three decades after the series began, is the only remaining member of the original cast to appear on the show.

The success of Casualty saw a number of spin-off series, the most notable of which was *Holby City*, which first aired in 1999 and took its title from the name of the hospital in which both dramas are set. There was also the short-lived *HolbyBlue*, the hybrid spin-off *Casualty@Holby City* and the period mini-series *Casualty 1906, Casualty 1907* and *Casualty 1909*.

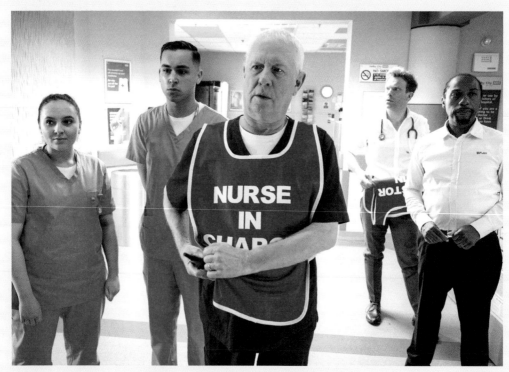

With Charlie Fairhead leading the way, the *Casualty* team brace themselves for the next emergency.

HIDING IN PLAIN SIGHT

Alongside well-known recurring characters, *Casualty* has featured actors who are famous for other roles in TV and film. For some of them, their appearance in *Casualty* occurred before they became a household name elsewhere. Can you spot 11 of these actors 'hiding in plain sight' in this wordsearch? Some clues to their identities are below.

1. Angie Watts in BBC soap *EastEnders* (5, 6)
2. Celia in *Calendar Girls* (5, 5)
3. Co-creator of BBC comedy *Little Britain* (5, 8)
4. Dr John Watson in BBC drama *Sherlock* (6, 7)
5. Emily in *Friends* and Rachel in BBC's *Cold Feet* (5, 9)
6. Loki in the *Avengers* film series and Jonathan Pine in BBC drama *The Night Manager* (3, 10)
7. Manuel in the BBC comedy *Fawlty Towers* (6, 5)
8. Rose in the film *Titanic* (4, 7)
9. Sybil in the BBC comedy *Fawlty Towers* (8, 6)
10. The ninth Doctor in BBC's *Doctor Who* (11, 9)
11. Will Turner in the *Pirates of the Caribbean* film series (7, 5)

```
S E L A C S A L L E N U R P M
H K F N I R G K X Z K L T O E
C J E W O O S H L A T O O M L
A U Z I Z S R Y T P M L A Z A
S G R S P A B E H H B R W D D
W Q S J U G W O I O T H C A N
E M R Z E I D D D I W E Y Q E
R B X E N Q D N N A L K T Y X
D T I S H L A F N I T R S Z A
N D L Y E L R D A B G I N E B
A E T S R E S I I Z O X N V N
T N T O E B M T W G Q P N A E
S O Y M Q R I T P I Z C K N L
N D A V I D W A L L I A M S E
T N L E O V R P H V X X D A H
```

STAFF LIST

Some of the characters who appeared in *Casualty* in 2021 are shown below, with their names and job titles given beneath their photos. Each of the job titles, however, has had all of the letters of 'CASUALTY' removed. Fill in the letters – one letter per gap – to restore the full staff list.

Connie Beauchamp
_ _ INI _ _ _   _ E _ D

Charlie Fairhead
EMERGEN _ _ N _ R _ E

Dylan Keogh
_ ON _ _ _ _ _ N _

Ethan Hardy
REGI _ _ R _ R

Iain Dean
P _ R _ MEDI _

Jade Lovall
_ _ _ FF   N _ R _ E

Jan Jenning
D _ _ _   M _ N _ GER

Marty Kirkby
_ _ _ DEN _   N _ R _ E

Rash Masum
J _ NIOR   DO _ _ OR

103

THE ARCHERS

Ask someone unfamiliar with the world's longest-running drama where the village of Ambridge in the English county of Borsetshire is and they may look at you strangely. Neither can be found on a map. And yet they have been a mainstay of a particular aspect of British culture for over 70 years.

Those wishing to know what the world of *The Archers* looks like could travel the area between Worcestershire and Warwickshire, south of the city of Birmingham, in what is known as the Midlands. That's where the drama is set. But listeners will be more familiar with fictional places like the county town of Borchester and nearby city of Felpersham.

The series has recorded daily life for generations of people living in and around the Archers' family farm Brookfield, along with life on neighbouring farms and nearby towns. It was created as a series of pilot episodes by Godfrey Basely in 1950, before it became five 15-minute weekly episodes in 1951. (Since 1998, it has been six 12½-minute episodes.)

Originally intended as a way of educating farmers after the Second World War, the show soon grew in popularity. Though existing within its own bubble, the series has engaged with current affairs, from the 9/11 attacks to the impact of the COVID-19 pandemic. And going against the grain of its folksy image, the series has often tackled serious themes, from controversial farming practices such as genetically modified crops and animal culling to drug addiction and sexual assault. And it has featured an impressive array of guest appearances over the years, from sports and screen figures to members of the royal family.

More than 19,500 episodes of *The Archers* have been broadcast since the show was first aired in 1951.

HOME SWEET HOME

All but four of the place names listed below are fictional locations in *The Archers*. Which four? Then, can you match each fictional place that does feature with its description on the right? For bonus points, can you also say what connects the four locations that do not appear in *The Archers* to the show?

Ambridge	A fictional village
Barwick Green	A fictional village
Borchester	The county in which *The Archers* is set
Borsetshire	The county town
Brookfield	The farm owned by the Aldridge family
Cutnall Green	The farm owned by the Archer family
Felpersham	The main village
Hanbury	The nearest city to Ambridge
Home Farm	The pub
Inkberrow	The stately home owned by the Pargetter family
Lower Loxley Hall	
Loxley Barrett	
Penny Hassett	
The Bull	

HIDDEN TALENTS

All of these famous faces have lent their voices to guest appearances on *The Archers* over the years. Can you name the person in each image and match them to the storyline they were involved in, below?

- Appeared as themself, in a 'radio on the radio'
- Appeared as themself, prompting a previously silent character to break their silence
- Appeared in an episode commemorating the NSPCC
- Appeared in association with the National Osteoporosis Society, of which they are a patron
- Appeared in the 10,000th episode as a character who has previously always been silent
- Appeared in The Bull as a suspected 'mystery judge' for a Pub of the Year competition
- Judged entries from the villagers of Ambridge in the National Gardens Scheme
- Presented prizes at an Ambridge Sport Relief contest

Sport

Broadcast media transformed the way we consume sport, bringing weekly matches into the home and introducing the world to a vast spectrum of competitive activities. Sporting events also gave broadcasters the opportunity to push the limits of technology, through outside and live programming. With the increasing sophistication of analogue and then digital equipment, they were able to capture sporting events at an ever-impressive level. The BBC led the way, covering all manner of sports, from weekly football matches and the FA and World Cup finals, Ascot and the Grand National, and the annual Oxbridge Boat Race, to the full panoply of events at both the Summer and Winter Olympics. It expanded its programming to include magazine programmes covering all events and specific shows catering to the most popular sports.

SPORTS REGULARS

As coverage of sporting events increased, programming schedules made way for shows dedicated to one sport or more general overviews of the sporting world. Along with these came a wave of presenters whose personalities – and idiosyncrasies – became inextricably linked with the sport they covered. Many were previously champions in their field.

The first major sports show on the BBC was *Sportsview*, which began airing in 1954 and immediately became a sensation when, by chance, it captured Roger Bannister breaking the four-minute mile. The show was hosted first by Peter Dimmock, and then Frank Bough, who would become synonymous with *Grandstand*. Launching on 11 October 1958 and dominating the Saturday afternoon schedule, *Grandstand* became British television's flagship weekly sports programme. David Coleman was the main host for a decade. When Bough took over in 1968, Coleman moved to *Sportsview*, which later that year became *Sportsnight*. Under Bough, *Grandstand* covered every major sport and event. It remained on air – even expanding to a *Sunday Grandstand* edition – until 2007, with subsequent presenters including Des Lynam and Steve Rider.

Other programmes focused on individual sports, with commentators who would become celebrities in their own field. They included the snooker programme *Pot Black*, commissioned by David Attenborough to coincide with the arrival of colour. Its presenter was David Vine with Ted Lowe commentating. Peter Alliss oversaw golfing tournaments, Murray Walker's voice accompanied Formula One, Eddie Waring was the voice of rugby league, while Bill McLaren and Cliff Morgan were associated with rugby union. Ron Pickering was the voice of athletics, while Sue Carpenter and Harry Carpenter dominated coverage of tennis and boxing. And with football and its main round-up show *Match of the Day*, Jimmy Hill, Gary Lineker and a host of ex-footballers remained in the world of the beautiful game by commentating on it.

Two familiar faces from BBC sport, Sue Barker (left), long-time host of *A Question of Sport*, and Murray Walker (above), the voice of Formula One.

GAME SET MATCH

Draw horizontal and vertical lines to join the equipment below into pairs, so that each pair contains one piece of sporting equipment and one microphone. Lines cannot cross either another line or any item.

SPORTING CHANCES

Each of these sporting stars went on to become a presenter or commentator on a BBC programme, covering the sport they used to play. Can you name the person in each photo, then match them with the BBC show they are most associated with presenting from the list given here?

- *Match of the Day*
- *Ski Sunday*
- *Test Match Special*
- *Today at Wimbledon*

MATCH OF THE DAY

The longest-running television football programme in the world, *Match of the Day* was one of the roster of programmes commissioned by David Attenborough when he was appointed Controller of BBC Two in 1965. One of the most revered sporting programmes today, it was not entirely welcome when it first launched, particularly by the Football Association, who feared a drop in gate attendances.

On 22 August 1964, Kenneth Wolstenholme welcomed audiences to the first episode of the show from the centre of the pitch at Anfield. Back then, the show's remit was to present 'the highlights of a top match in today's Football League programme'. Previously, only the FA Cup final and the odd game had ever been shown on television. A summary of Liverpool playing from home against Arsenal was a landmark in coverage of the

sport. According to David Attenborough, 'BBC Two managed to persuade the FA to let it do it, on the basis that nobody watched BBC Two'. But the show's audience gradually grew.

Match of the Day changed to colour on 15 November 1969, when Liverpool played West Ham United. And on 15 August 1970, Barry Stoller's iconic tune became the show's theme. A year later, audiences were able to see key moments in slow motion, which would have a significant impact on the way the game was analysed and referees' decisions were discussed. In the decades since, the show has come to be seen as an essential part of the football season.

Not one, but two football legends: *Match of the Day* stalwart Jimmy Hill (above) and former Arsenal forward and football pundit Ian Wright.

KEEPY-UPPY

Listed below in the left-hand column are the encoded names of the six English football clubs that have never been relegated from the Premier League. In the middle column is the top goal scorer for each of these clubs and then, in the right-hand column, the name of a football stadium historically associated with each club. Can you identify these six clubs, goal scorers and grounds – and their 2021 Premier League positions?

In each set of three matching items (club + player + stadium) the letters have been shifted forwards a consistent amount through the alphabet, according to the team's finishing position in the 2021 Premier League season. For example, West Ham finished 6th, so if this was one of the teams then its letters would have moved six places forward to become Ckyz Wgs, where W has become C (wrapping around from Z back to A), e has become k, and so on.

Clubs	Top Goal Scorers	Famous Grounds
Izamvit	Nshso Nokx	Dqilhog
Glipwie	Jvero Peqtevh	Qyynscyx Zkbu
Ofobdyx	Ldq Uxvk	Pqopjczg
Olyhusrro	Qpttf Nylhclz	Qnf Vtchhqtf
Ocpejguvgt Wpkvgf	Bpqmzzg Pmvzg	Wxeqjsvh Fvmhki
Avaaluoht Ovazwby	Ycapg Tqqpga	Dopal Ohya Shul

ON THE BALL

Solve each clue to reveal a word with the given number of letters, using only the letters found on the ball below. Every answer includes the letter in the middle of the ball, 'L'.

Capped Welsh footballer, Gareth . . . (4)
League results are tallied in this (5)
Anatomical term for the lower leg bones (7)
Everton and Chelsea home colour (4)
Energy source (4)
A word frequently used to describe the game of football (9)

LIVE SPORTS COVERAGE

Sports coverage has been one of the staples of BBC's programming since its inception. As audio and visual technology developed, the ability of the broadcaster to offer audiences coverage of a wide range of sporting activities increased, from weekly fixtures to larger international events.

Competition between broadcasters over subsequent decades has often been as challenging as the sports themselves, with contracts for various sports and events changing hands every few years. Nevertheless, the BBC has remained one of the leading broadcasters of live sporting events around the world.

On 15 January 1927, the BBC aired its first live sports broadcast, radio coverage of the rugby union international game between England and Wales. A week later, on 15 January, Arsenal's home league fixture against Sheffield United became the first live football match to be broadcast. The first outside television broadcast took place on 2 June 1931, with coverage of the Epsom Derby. Racing from Ascot began in 1951, while fans of the Grand National would have to wait until 1960 for it to be televised.

On 21 June 1937, the Wimbledon Tennis Championships aired for the first time. A year later, on 30 April 1938, the first televised coverage of the FA Cup took place. The Second World War interrupted all sports transmissions. They returned in 1946 with coverage of Wimbledon and cricket, and then, two years later, wide coverage of the London Olympics. However, it wasn't until 1954 that the FIFA World Cup was televised in the United Kingdom. In the same year, the BBC Sports Personality of the Year award was introduced.

Sports presenter Clare Balding (above); the Oxford and Cambridge University Boat Race (below), first televised by the BBC on 2 April 1938.

SOME QUESTIONS OF SPORT

How many of the following British sporting
questions can you answer?

1. Between which two bridges on the Thames is
   the Boat Race raced?

2. Who won the first-ever women's gold medal for
   Olympic boxing, in 2012?

3. In what year did Andy Murray win his first
   Wimbledon Championship?

4. Who bowled the Super Over in 2019 which won
   England the men's Cricket World Cup?

5. Which England player kicked the goal that won
   the team's first-ever Rugby World Cup?

6. Which cyclist became the first British man to win
   the Tour de France, in 2012?

7. How many medals did Chris Hoy win in the 2012
   London Olympics?

8. Which Team GB athlete won gold in the 800m and
   1500m events at the 2004 Athens Olympics?

9. Between which years did Lewis Hamilton win four
   consecutive World Driver's Championship titles?

10. What do the four pictured athletes all have
    in common?

Music

Even if Dame Nellie Melba hadn't performed an aria on the UK's first live radio broadcast, it wouldn't have taken long for someone to see the potential of radio to champion the music world. In keeping with the times, for its first few decades, music programming on BBC radio was a strictly conservative affair. A diet of classical and light music was the order of the day, even with the rise in popular music following the Second World War and the arrival of rock and roll in the mid-1950s. The threat of independent radio brought in a seismic change. Although laws were introduced to shut down pirate radio stations, their popularity did not go unnoticed at the BBC and the creation of Radio 1 in 1967 changed everything. It not only embraced the rapidly changing world of rock and pop, but made the Disc Jockey a celebrity – the radio host's personality often informing the choice of music as much as audience tastes.

TOP OF THE POPS

The music chart show format had already been a hit in the United States with *American Bandstand*, which first aired in 1958. Considering the huge impact of British bands and pop singers from the early 1960s onwards, it was no surprise that a similar format would appeal to British audiences. BBC producer Johnnie Stewart came up with the idea of *Top of the Pops*, which would remain on air for more than 40 years, becoming the world's longest-running weekly music show.

The show first aired on 1 January 1964, opening with Dusty Springfield performing 'I Only Want to Be With You', followed by the Rolling Stones and 'I Wanna Be Your Man'. It ended with The Beatles performing that week's No. 1 track 'I Want to Hold Your Hand'. The last band to play on the final programme, on 30 July 2006, was Snow Patrol with their track 'Chasing Cars'.

Johnnie Stewart introduced a number of house rules that were mostly adhered to for the course of the show's duration. It would always end with the No. 1 song for that week, which was also the only record that could be played on consecutive weeks. The highest new entry would play, along with the highest new climber. Songs that were descending the charts were never featured.

Miming to a track was initially used, before bands were allowed to use a backing track – or in-house orchestra for solo artists – while the singer performed live. The arrival of the music video in the late 1970s significantly changed the format, but it was the shift to digital and new ways of collecting listening data that spelled the end of the show. It continues to exist as the archive programme *TOTP2*.

Elton John (above) and Becky Hill (left). It seems glittery clothing has long been associated with the glamour of performing on *Top of the Pops*.

CHANGE OF KEY

The names of five artists who have appeared on *Top of the Pops*, and one song title, have been disguised below by 'changing their key' in some way that it is up to you to work out. Can you crack the codes and then match each name to its corresponding *TOTP* fact below?

Disguised names:

1. BLIEE RIBHGRC

2. MGFFID MGY

3. SDRFD FGINSAOURF

4. FRDDN CGY

5. THD ADGTLDS

6. OGSIS

TOTP Facts:

A. A performance of this song by Rod Stewart featured radio DJ John Peel miming on the mandolin

B. This artist appeared the most on the show, with nearly 160 performances

C. This band is credited with the longest single performance on the show, at over nine minutes

D. This band performed live on the show, but the recording of their performance was unfortunately deleted

E. This band has two brothers who once switched places for a mimed performance

F. This French artist's No. 1 single, with Jane Birkin, was banned from *Top of the Pops*

MISSING NOTES

Each of the tracks that appeared on *Top of the Pops*, below, spent at least two consecutive weeks at No. 1 in the UK singles chart. Each line contains the name of a song and its corresponding artist, plus the year of its original release – but only their initials are shown. Can you identify each of the songs and its performer? And which one holds the record for the most consecutive weeks spent as the UK's No. 1?

(E I D) I D I F Y by B A (1991)

B R by Q (1975)

D Y R W T H M by C C (1982)

L I A A by W W W (1994)

R by F G T H (1984)

Y T F, T L, M E by B W (1974; performed in 2000 on TOTP2)

LATER... WITH JOOLS HOLLAND

Performed as live but recorded a few days in advance of broadcast, *Later... with Jools Holland* is a relaxed music show presented by the former member of the band Squeeze and an accomplished pianist. It was originally created as an offshoot of the late-night arts magazine programme *The Late Show*, but has come to be embraced as one of the most popular, enduring and universally appealing television music shows.

The show helped forge Holland's image as an elder statesman of music television shows, a marked contrast to his earlier profile as one of the outspoken, occasionally profane, but entertaining presenters of the Channel 4 music magazine series *The Tube*. *Later...* reflects Holland's wide-ranging taste in music and champions emerging as well as established talent. The format is simple: a large, open studio features an audience of around 300 people and approximately five performing spaces. Holland moves between each, introducing and talking to the acts before they perform. And each episode opens with a short jam, featuring Holland and many of the guests. Holland also accompanies some performances on piano.

There is no specific musical theme to an episode, so a drill rapper might follow a pop group and come before a folk singer. Likewise, from the outset the show has proved to be refreshingly egalitarian, championing music from every corner of the world, no matter the genre. The popularity of the show in its first year led to *Jools' Annual Hootenanny*, a New Year's musical celebration, which first aired on 31 December 1993.

A typical *Later...* line-up: From left to right (top), FKA twigs, Brittany Howard, Noel Gallagher; (bottom) Harry Styles, Tom Jones, Jools, Abdullah Ibrahim.

EMERGING ARTISTS

Each of the clues below solves to reveal the one-word name of a band or artist who has appeared on *Later... with Jools Holland*. Can you solve the clues and then find the 'emerging' artists in the grid below? Names in the grid may be written in any direction.

A play's actors (4)
Abdomen, informally (5)
Arm joint (5)
Body's outer covering (4)
Cheese accompaniment (7)
Chirrup (5)
Conflicts between armies (7)
Cooked in oil (5)
Deletion (7)
Desert spring (5)
Difficult (6)
Disguised (9)
Extremely famous person (9)
Fire remnant (3)
Frequently occurring (6)
Hairy and unkempt (6)

Hollowed-out ground (4)
Hug (7)
Inactive pill (7)
Inhabitant of the Blue Planet, perhaps (9)
Insanity (7)
Jean material (5)
Lebanon's capital (6)
Loud horns (7)
Marine mammal (4)
Mythical queen of Carthage (4)
Newspaper heads (7)
Norway's capital (4)
Offshore coral structure (4)
One who nourishes (6)
Pain-relieving drug (8)

Portable breathing kit for divers (8)
Puree (4)
Red precious gem (4)
Roads (7)
Rubbish, in the US (7)
Smear (4)
Snake-like fishes (4)
Spiritual teacher (4)
Sportsperson (7)
Stinging sea creature (9)
Stream of liquid (3)
Throne claimants (10)
Typically white pigeon-like birds (5)
US state (5)
Vehicle congestions (7)
Velvety leather (5)
Venom-injecting barb (5)
Where *Later...* appears (10)
Young horses (5)

```
M M I F O E A M O R P H I N E L A F Y
I D P L E K A Q Q E F B O R E E L S Y
P R S B M E L R U A D J Z R S L W E H
C O M M O N D A T A Q I F Z K O D O V
M A D N E S S E X H L S T R E E T S R
A O V U J P T G R O L U X O U I H V T
A T A Q G U R U B O N I N S R X E E T
T C F S R S I E A L G S N G B S J E E
H B O L I X C B T W E E T G E E P P X
L O A R N S K H T E F T H V C U L U A
E S L E C B Y A L M N S O A R S A L S
T A S E O L R T E O I D R Q B K C P Y
E R S F G U U Q S F Q B E F R I E D C
E D N T N R B T Y G M K W R L N B U R
L E F Y I I Y L T E L E V I S I O N A
B N X E T N L S H A G G Y L C A S T C
O I B S O E G K S U M U A F D I D O K
W M C H J E R A S U R E G A R B A G E
T R A F F I C D C R S U P E R S T A R
```

BBC PROMS

The Proms have become a world-renowned institution, presenting some of the finest conductors, performers and orchestras – alongside the BBC Symphony Orchestra – across their wide and diverse summer programme. Conceived independently, The Proms have been synonymous with the BBC since the organization took over running the concerts in 1927.

The brainchild of impresario Robert Newman, who wanted to reach a wider audience with a series of programmes that balanced popular and challenging classical works, The Proms first took place in London's recently opened Queen's Hall on 10 August 1895. Henry Wood was brought on as conductor of the hall's permanent orchestra and the first Proms season. He would remain in that position until his death in 1944, shortly after he conducted his 50th season.

The BBC took over The Proms when a lack of funding threatened the classical programme. In 1930, the BBC Symphony Orchestra was founded. The Proms remained at the Queen's Hall until it was destroyed in a Luftwaffe bomb attack on 10 May 1941. The event subsequently moved to the Royal Albert Hall, now its permanent home. The format and the remit of The Proms has remained consistent, balancing new and experimental works with a popular programme. The audience comprises those who have booked seats and the 'promenaders' who queue on the day to buy cheap tickets to the performances. *The Last Night of the Proms* has become a highlight of the BBC's televised programming of the season (most concerts are live on radio), with the music programme of the latter half remaining faithful to the format introduced by Sir Malcolm Sargent in 1954, during his tenure as chief conductor.

CBeebies presenters perform *A Musical Trip to the Moon* (above); Katherine Jenkins performs at BBC Proms in the Park, Hyde Park, 2009 (right).

LAST NIGHT AT THE PROMS

The names of six orchestral instruments have been blended with the names of six musical pieces traditionally played on *The Last Night of the Proms*. The letters are in the correct order for every word, but it's up to you to work out how they have been blended. Spaces and punctuation have been removed. Can you uncover the six famous pieces, and the six instruments?

JTEIRMUPSAANLIEM

CALUALRDILNANEGSTYNE

LTANDROOFMHOPBEAONNDGELORY

FANXTASYIALONBORIPTIHSHOSEANSEONGS

GRLUOLCEKBERNISTAPINNEIAL

BGODASAVSETHSEQOUEONEN

TRUE AND FALSE

First, work out which of the following statements about The Proms are true, and which are false. If you have answered correctly then the numbers next to each chosen answer will add up to 49, the number of proms in the very first season back in 1895.

A. **Smoking is permitted at The Proms (TRUE 12, FALSE 17)**

B. **Lying down is permitted whilst attending The Proms (TRUE 8, FALSE 5)**

C. **The only object to survive the bombing of Queens' Hall was a bronze statue of Henry Wood (TRUE 3, FALSE 9)**

D. **French electronic duo Daft Punk have performed at The Proms (TRUE 15, FALSE 11)**

E. ***The Last Night of the Proms* had its first female conductor in 1984 (TRUE 13, FALSE 4)**

F. **The Proms were halted completely for several years during the Second World War (TRUE 6, FALSE 1)**

G. **Sir Henry Wood once presented a piece by a 'Paul Klenovsky' – but it was in fact a Bach piece he had arranged himself (TRUE 5, FALSE 8)**

LIVE AID

One of the largest television broadcasts of all time, watched by approximately 1.9 billion people across 150 countries, or 40 per cent of the world population, the genesis of Live Aid was BBC journalist Michael Buerk's news report in 1984 of the Ethiopia famine. His stark and moving account of the scale of the situation became a landmark in crisis reporting and its impact prompted the recording and release of the charity single 'Do They Know It's Christmas', which in turn led to Live Aid.

The Boomtown Rats and Ultravox band leaders Bob Geldof and Midge Ure were responsible for corralling a variety of stars to perform the single. Shortly after, Culture Club singer Boy George suggested to Geldof the idea of a fundraising concert. Geldof soon developed it into a transatlantic venture, with the first concert starting in Wembley Stadium before a second began at the John F. Kennedy Stadium in Philadelphia. Both concerts featured a variety of the most popular and established rock and pop acts of the time. (Subsequent concerts in this vein would broaden their remit to include artists from nations outside of Europe and the United States.)

The BBC was responsible for recording, filming and transmission of the ten-hour Wembley concert. The most ambitious international satellite television event at that time, it was recorded in mono for TV and in stereo for radio, and featured a small army of British TV presenters and radio disc jockeys throughout the day. The success of the event inspired subsequent charity concerts around the world.

With an attendance of 72,000 at Wembley (above) and 89,500 in Philadelphia, Live Aid raised £125 million in famine relief for Africa.

LAST MAN SINGING

All of the following singers performed at the Live Aid concert in Wembley Stadium, but which of them was the last billed artist to perform, prior to the finale? Reveal the answer by finding out which of the singers cannot be found in the wordsearch grid beneath. The names may be written in any direction, either forwards or backwards, including diagonally.

ADAM ANT
BOB GELDOF
BONO
BRYAN FERRY
DAVID BOWIE
ELTON JOHN
ELVIS COSTELLO
FREDDIE MERCURY
GEORGE MICHAEL
HOWARD JONES
MIDGE URE
NIK KERSHAW
PAUL MCCARTNEY
PHIL COLLINS
ROGER DALTREY
STING

E	L	V	I	S	C	O	S	T	E	L	L	O	Y
S	R	W	A	H	S	R	E	K	K	I	N	R	B
E	B	O	R	E	L	I	O	R	E	E	U	B	S
N	R	L	G	I	I	G	G	R	T	C	O	N	E
O	Y	B	O	E	H	W	U	D	R	B	I	E	E
J	A	D	O	I	R	E	O	E	M	L	I	L	E
D	N	A	I	B	G	D	M	B	L	M	T	N	T
R	F	U	O	D	G	E	A	O	D	O	E	N	Y
A	E	O	I	L	I	E	C	L	N	I	A	E	S
W	R	M	N	D	O	L	L	J	T	M	V	T	E
O	R	R	D	O	I	A	O	D	A	R	I	A	E
H	Y	E	M	H	B	H	R	D	O	N	E	R	D
A	R	Y	P	E	N	A	A	R	G	F	E	Y	I
F	G	E	O	R	G	E	M	I	C	H	A	E	L

ALL IN ORDER

Listed below are eight bands and artists who performed at some point during the ten-hour concert at Wembley. Use the clues beneath, and your logical deduction skills, to number each of them by the order in which they appeared on stage.

- The Boomtown Rats were not the first band to appear
- Elvis Costello sang immediately after Spandau Ballet
- Sade sang later than Spandau Ballet but earlier than Queen
- Status Quo performed earlier than Spandau Ballet
- The Who performed later than Sade
- Dire Straits performed immediately before Queen
- Elvis Costello appeared later than the Boomtown Rats, but earlier than Queen
- Queen were not the last band to perform from this group

___ **BOOMTOWN RATS**

___ **DIRE STRAITS**

___ **ELVIS COSTELLO**

___ **QUEEN**

___ **SADE**

___ **SPANDAU BALLET**

___ **STATUS QUO**

___ **THE WHO**

DISC JOCKEYS

A disc jockey adds colour and character to a radio show – less a bridge between a playlist of songs than a personality that sets the tone for a programme. From the effervescence of a morning host to more laid back afternoon programming and late night introspection – this last best characterized by the legendary tones of John Peel and 'whispering' Bob Harris – their presence at the BBC grew following the disbanding of pirate radio stations in the late 1960s. Before long, they played an essential role in attracting audiences.

Even by the mid-1960s, there remained a conservatism within BBC Radio. Popular music was barely represented. But times were changing and in 1967 it was clear to Robin Scott, the controller of recently created stations Radio 1 and Radio 2, that a new breed of presenter was required. Scott attracted DJs who had worked with popular pirate stations such as Radio Caroline. Together, they not only championed current popular music, their on-air banter radically transformed the previously formal tone of the broadcaster's output.

Chris Evans

John Peel

In contrast to the pirate stations, rules regarding decorum would remain – as evidenced by Kenny Everett's being removed from air in 1970 for making a comment about the minister for transport's wife, and the 'Sachsgate' controversy involving Jonathan Ross and Russell Brand in 2008. Nevertheless, many became household names, including Tony Blackburn, Pete Murray, Terry Wogan, Jimmy Young, Tommy Vance, Johnny Walker and John Peel, with Annie Nightingale becoming Radio 1's first female DJ in 1970. While the disc jockey's status has changed over the years, the Radio 1 breakfast slot remains one of the holy grails for those with ambition.

Liam Gallagher presents Annie Nightingale with a Guinness World Record – for the longest career as a female radio presenter (40 years in 2010).

THE FACE BEHIND THE MIC

Pictured below are all the Radio 1 DJs who have hosted the breakfast show for at least two years. Can you match each name to a face at the bottom of the page?

When the images are arranged in chronological order of hosting tenure, the additional letters in the bottom left-hand corner of each image will spell out the surname of a legendary BBC DJ.

- **Chris Moyles**
- **Dave Lee Travis**
- **Greg James**
- **Mike Read**
- **Mike Smith**
- **Nick Grimshaw**
- **Noel Edmonds**
- **Sara Cox**
- **Simon Mayo**
- **Tony Blackburn**
- **Zoe Ball**

Factual

Lord Reith could not have foreseen how fully his vision would be embraced by the broadcaster and its audience, for the BBC to inform and educate as well as entertain. Radio, and then TV, shows engaged with the wider world on a scale hitherto unseen. Just as communication had made the planet a smaller place, broadcasting brought every corner of the globe to audiences with startling, detailed clarity. From the annals of history through to the micro and macrocosm of our universe, and from advances in technology to the various faces of art, culture and human affairs, factual programming became a staple of both radio and television. It ranged from magazine programmes that ran the gamut, from the political and personal to advances in science, to blockbuster series that not only enlightened a mass audience, but became landmarks in the history of broadcasting.

LANDMARK FACTUAL SHOWS

BBC TV has regularly commissioned large-scale series that grapple with vast and complex subjects. These landmark productions have influenced countless other programmes and stand as a testament to the power of television.

The Great War (1964) was commissioned to commemorate the 50th anniversary of the outbreak of the First World War. The epic 26-episode series employed archive footage, interviews and staged re-enactments to detail the progress of events, the experiences of soldiers and horrors of the battlefield. It would set the standard for the historical documentary series format, which would be copied a decade later for Thames Television's *The World at War* (1973–74). Subsequent acclaimed series detailing the impact of conflict include the award-winning *The Nazis: A Warning from History* (1997), *The Death of Yugoslavia* (1995), which grappled with the complexity of the collapse of the Balkan country, and *Once Upon a Time in Iraq* (2020), which detailed the 2003 invasion and its aftermath through the experiences of journalists, military personnel and Iraqi citizens.

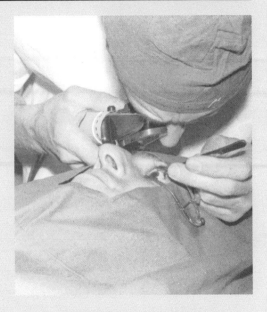

The Ascent of Man (1973) traced the history of human society through scientific development. The series, presented by mathematician and historian Jacob Bronowski, was inspired by the earlier *Civilisation* (1969), a history of the development of art, created and presented by Kenneth Clark. Both series were commissioned by David Attenborough when he was head of BBC Two and who would also go on to present his own landmark series *Life on Earth*.

If *Civilisation* looked at the development of classical art, Robert Hughes' *The Shock of the New* analysed the impact of modern art since the Impressionists on culture and society. It's a title that would perfectly suit Adam Curtis, a unique filmmaker, whose body of work explores the mechanisms that control society, most notably a post-9/11 world with his unsettling films *The Power of Nightmares*, *Bitter Lake* and *Can't Get You Out of My Head*.

With shows like *Life on Earth* (left) and *Tomorrow's World* (above), the BBC gave audiences insights into otherwise unexplored territory.

THE ASCENT OF MAN

All 13 episode titles in the series *The Ascent of Man* have been split up below, with the first part of each title on the left and the second part on the right. Reunite the episode titles by joining the dots with straight lines.

Once paired up correctly, read the crossed-through letters from top to bottom to reveal the name of an actor who lent his voice to the epilogues when the show was first broadcast in the United States.

Generation upon ●	● Childhood
Knowledge ●	● Clockwork
Lower than ●	● for Power
Music of ●	● Generation
The Drive ●	● Messenger
The Grain in ●	● of Creation
The Harvest of ●	● or Certainty
The Hidden ●	● Structure
The Ladder ●	● the Angels
The Long ●	● the Seasons
The Majestic ●	● the Spheres
The Starry ●	● the Stone
World within ●	● World

THE SHOCK OF THE NEW

Can you find the name of an iconic artwork, featured in an episode of *The Shock of the New*, on the palette opposite? Each letter should be used exactly once.

As a clue, the artist's name is given here, though it is missing some letters:

P _ _ _ O P _ _ _ _ _ O

In addition, there are at least 50 further words that can be created from this art palette. By using the centre letter (R), plus two or more of the other letters no more than once each, how many can you find?

MASTERMIND

Less a conventional TV gameshow format than an assault course for grey matter, the popularity of *Mastermind* saw it catapult from a marginal late-night slot to prime-time BBC One. It was created by a former RAF gunner, with a format that drew on his experiences as a prisoner of war.

When caught by German forces during the Second World War, TV producer Bill Wright was constantly asked three questions: name, rank and number. That informed the introduction of each contestant on the show, where they would be asked for their name, occupation and specialist subject. From there, *Mastermind* was split into two rounds. Sitting in the, now iconic, black leather chair, each of the four contestants on every episode first answered two minutes of questions on their topic of choice. Then each would answer two-and-a-half minutes of general knowledge questions. The winner, who receives an engraved glass bowl, is the contestant with the highest score.

Each episode, which opens with the theme 'Approaching Menace' by British composer Neil Richardson, took place in a different location, with the first filmed in Liverpool University and aired on 11 September 1972. Its host was Magnus Magnusson, who became known for the catchphrase 'I've started, so I'll finish', which was spoken whenever time ran out while he was reading the last question in a round. He remained as host until 1997, when he retired and BBC One cancelled the show. It moved to Radio 4 between 1998 and 2000 and was hosted by Peter Snow, before Clive Anderson took over for a brief stint in 2001 on the Discovery Channel. *Mastermind* returned to the BBC in 2003 and was hosted by John Humphrys, before he stepped down in 2021 to be replaced by Clive Myrie.

Magnus Magnusson, the show's host for 25 years, pictured here with the iconic black chair.

I'VE STARTED, SO I'LL FINISH

Listed below are the first halves of various specialist subjects chosen by *Mastermind* champions. The second halves of each subject are then hidden in the wordsearch grid.

Can you work out what they are and then find them all? The subjects consist of two words each, and their second halves may be written in any direction in the grid.

Abraham
Academy
Doctor
Édith
Empress
Father
Francis
Grand
Nancy
Olympic
Otis
Romanov
Shakespeare's
Solar
Westminster

R	P	D	G	N	I	D	D	E	R	F
D	L	F	Y	B	S	R	B	S	U	W
Y	E	N	E	S	Y	A	L	P	C	N
T	U	T	B	F	S	K	O	D	X	L
S	G	Y	B	I	T	E	P	Z	P	O
A	A	N	A	Q	E	U	E	M	H	C
N	J	W	I	S	M	W	R	W	A	N
Y	P	O	A	C	T	J	A	N	I	I
D	I	O	X	R	N	O	A	Y	V	L
G	A	Q	V	J	D	E	R	Z	I	V
H	F	K	U	T	H	S	F	U	L	Z

SPECIALIST SUBJECT: THE BBC

The solutions to many of the following questions can be found in this very book. How many can you answer in a minute?

1. In what year was the original Live Aid concert broadcast on the BBC?
2. What kind of animal was the Blue Peter pet, Joey?
3. What name is given to the pre-recorded show hosted by Jools Holland, broadcast on New Year's Eve?
4. An enamelled pear blossom made by which Russian jeweller was valued at £1 million on an episode of *Antiques Roadshow*?
5. Which London concert hall is the permanent home of The Proms?
6. What is the surname of the main family in *Peaky Blinders*?
7. What type of plane did *Tomorrow's World* presenter Raymond Baxter fly during the Second World War?
8. Tess Daly and which veteran entertainer were the original presenters of *Strictly Come Dancing*?
9. What is the name of the public house on Albert Square which features frequently in *EastEnders*?
10. In what fictional county is *The Archers* set?

ONLY CONNECT

Giving *Mastermind* a run for its money as the most cerebrally challenging television quiz show, *Only Connect* pits two teams against each other in a challenge to find connections between seemingly unrelated clues. It first aired on 15 September 2008.

The show takes its title from a line in E.M. Forster's novel *Howards End*: 'Only connect the prose and the passion, and both will be exalted'. It is hosted by Victoria Coren Mitchell, who presents with a combination of dry wit, self-deprecation and sarcasm. Although elements of the series have changed over the years (the original use of Greek letters was replaced by ancient Egyptian hieroglyphs, for example), the structure of the game has remained pretty much the same. Two teams of three people work their way through four rounds. In the first, 'Connections', a team has forty seconds to find a link between a maximum of four clues. The more clues they need, the lower their score. In 'Sequences', each set of four clues forms a sequence, the team see a maximum of three and have to guess the fourth. In round three, 'Connecting Wall', a team must figure out the four connections that link four sets of four clues, before the final buzzer round, where teams are given a maximum of four puzzle topics and have to guess a word or phrase whose vowels have been removed.

Teams are encouraged to choose a name that reflects their interests or talents and their performance is often the target of Mitchell Coren's jibes. Originally airing on BBC Four, the show is now a popular fixture on BBC Two.

Victoria Coren Mitchell, the show's host.

CONNECTIONS

Can you work out what connects all four of the items on each line below?

1) Fruit   Wall   Pellet   Ghost

2) City   Architecture   Creator   Technic

3) Hammer   Bridge   Pedal   Key

4) Base   Product   Mean   Rational

CONNECTING WALL

Arrange the following words into four groups of four items, so each item is used exactly once. There are more than four items that can fit into some sets, but only one way to place all 16 items simultaneously.

Seed	Root	Ace	Desserts
Edge	Baseline	Leaf	Tuber
Lead	Advantage	Bulb	Stalk
Draw	Flower	Superiority	Slice

MISSING VOWELS

Can you identify all four items in each set below? In each case all of the vowels have been deleted, and the remaining letters have been respaced.

1) Classical music composers

   BTH VN   LG R   DV RK   CG

2) Sports

   JD   CH CK Y   RC HR Y   LT MTF RS B

MICHAEL PALIN'S TRAVELS

The man who once sold a dead parrot became a popular actor, successful writer and beloved traveller to all corners of the world. As part of *Monty Python's Flying Circus*, Michael Palin helped revolutionize television comedy. But it was his transformation into a globetrotting guide, in the third decade of his television career, that saw Palin's popularity skyrocket.

In 1980, Palin presented an episode of *Great Railway Journeys of the World*, entitled 'Confessions of a Trainspotter', which saw him travel from London to the Kyle of Lochalsh, in Scotland. (He would return to the series in 1994 for the episode 'Derry to Kerry'.) But it was an offer to travel the route that novelist Jules Verne created for his character Phileas Fogg that launched Palin's new career. *Around the World in 80 Days with Michael Palin* (1989)

was a whistle-stop tour that circumnavigated the world. Like Verne's character, Palin could not take a plane and was accompanied by a five-person film crew, who were collectively named 'Passepartout', after Fogg's manservant. Aside from the ravishing sights and entertaining setbacks experienced by the travellers, Palin's charisma and wonder at the sights he witnessed, along with his affability and willingness to engage with anyone, won over audiences.

Pole to Pole (1992) followed. Then came *Full Circle* (1997), *Hemingway Adventure* (1999), *Sahara* (2002), *Himalaya* (2004), *New Europe* (2007) and *Brazil* (2012). As with David Attenborough, Palin's distinct British sensibility, his charm, openness and boundless enthusiasm in every series, along with his intelligence and inquisitiveness have made him a singular figure on the landscape of television documentary.

Michael Palin poses in front of London's British Museum, home to many artefacts from sites visited by the traveller.

AROUND THE WORLD IN 80 STEPS

Some of the countries visited in *Around the World in 80 Days* are hidden in the grid opposite. Find your way around the world by tracing a path in the grid, moving horizontally or vertically between letters and spelling out names of countries as you go. Start your journey in the square pointed at by the arrow and finish on the star. All of the countries can be traced out in the same order they were visited by Palin, except for one. Which country is out of order?

U	G	D	O	M	E	G	Y
I	N	N	C	N	F	E	T	P
T	K	I	E	A	R	C	Q	A
E	D	U	A	R	E	E	A	T
R	T	S	Y	G	P	A	R	S
I	T	A	L	R	O	G	N	I
A	I	O	K	E	H	N	I	N
C	G	N	G	N	O	A	I	D
H	I	N	A	J	A	P	A	★

FULL CIRCLE

In *Full Circle*, Palin travelled anticlockwise around the Pacific Rim in a circle, starting from the Bering Strait. The names of some of the countries he visited have likewise been written anticlockwise in a circle, although each country has had one extra letter added.

When these extra letters are read in the same order as their corresponding countries were visited, they spell out the name of one of the countries Palin visited in the final episode. Can you identify each of the countries, including the extra country?

135

GREAT RAILWAY JOURNEYS

The perfect recipe for the armchair traveller places a celebrity and, more recently, a former politician on a notable rail journey to revel in the sights, sounds and personalities they encounter on their trip. Although the series' name and format has changed over the years, its mission in offering audiences a vicarious vacation remains the same.

The first series, entitled *Great Railway Journeys of the World*, first aired in 1980. It comprised seven episodes and featured as our guide Ludovic Kennedy, Michael Frayn, Brian Thompson, Michael Palin, Michael Wood, Miles Kington and Eric Robson. The journeys traversed six continents over the series. The most notable is arguably Michael Palin's, who made his way from London to the Kyle of Lochalsh in Scotland. The writer, actor and *Monty Python* team member proved such an affable screen presence that by the end of the decade he would embark on a new career as an intrepid television explorer. He would also appear in the second series, travelling from Derry in Northern Ireland to Kerry in the Republic of Ireland.

There was a 14-year hiatus before the series returned as *Great Railway Journeys*, with Clive Anderson as host. Two subsequent series followed in 1996 and 1999. In 2010, Michael Portillo – who hosted an episode of the fourth series, from Granada to Salamanca in Spain – began presenting *Great British Railway Journeys*. By 2021 it had run for 13 series and more than 240 episodes. He also hosted the off-shoot series *Great Continental Journeys* and *Great Asian Railway Journeys*.

Michael Portillo interviews the driver of the iconic steam locomotive *Flying Scotsman* before departing for Edinburgh from King's Cross station.

HERE TO THERE

Encoded below are the names of seven routes featured in the *Great Railway Journeys* series. Can you decode the place names and reveal the journeys? The starting points for each journey have been given in the left-hand column and the end points on the right, although the two lists are not in the same order. Seven different changes have been used to conceal the place names – one for each journey, with the start and end points of each journey having been manipulated in the same way. For example, 'St Petersburg to Tashkent' might have been changed by removing every second letter from each name, giving S PTRBR on the left and TSKN on the right – which could then be matched up to make one of the journeys. It is up to you to identify the seven different modification schemes.

ACCLTUAT		AAABQ
AELOPP		ARAJTSAHN
EFSSZ		LFSSZ
GRND	**TO**	ONKKGBA
KYOTO		RCADI
ONDO		SHIMAKAGO
SRPONIGEA		SLMNC

CREWE TO CREWE

In 1996, a comedian presented an episode of *Great Railway Journeys* that took them on a UK journey that both started and ended at Crewe. Can you join all of the dots below to form a looped route that reveals their name? The loop cannot cross or touch itself at any point, and only horizontal and vertical lines between dots are allowed. Some parts of the loop are already given. Once complete, read the letters that the loop passes through in order, clockwise from the star, to reveal the answer.

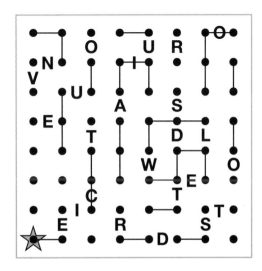

ANTIQUES ROADSHOW

Antiques Roadshow began as a sedate, late Sunday afternoon programme before rejuvenating into a popular prime-time show. This once fusty slice of British eccentricity hopped on to the coattails of the burgeoning home improvement trend in TV programming, becoming a repurposed antiquity for a modern audience.

The original show was hosted by Bruce Parker, then best known as one of the presenters on the current affairs programme *Nationwide*. He was joined in 1979 by newscaster Angela Rippon. Hugh Scully took over in 1981, presenting until 2000, when he was replaced by Michael Aspel. The current presenter, Fiona Bruce, took over in 2008. Over the years, there have been hundreds of experts, but few are as memorable as one of the earliest, Arthur Negus, who appeared on the show between 1979 and 1983. Over the years, the format for the show has been copied internationally, from various countries in Europe to the United States and Canada.

The show's origins lay in a 1977 documentary that saw members of a London auction house visiting properties in the West Country, evaluating items of potentially great historical or artistic import. A pilot of the show format was subsequently aired in May 1977. Recorded in Hereford, it proved hugely popular. The format has changed little since that first edition; members of the public bring items to be valued to wherever the show is being hosted that week and a small group of experts judge their worth. The reaction of the owners – either pleasant surprise at the value of the object they own, or disappointment at the news that it's worthless – is what makes the show so compelling.

Two much-loved faces of *Antiques Roadshow*, presenter Fiona Bruce (top left) and fount of antiques knowledge Arthur Negus (above).

COLLECTOR'S EDITION

Listed below are descriptions of six items featured on *Antiques Roadshow*. For each item, can you work out the person or entity **highlighted in bold** that gives each piece its unique value, and then match it to one of the upper estimates of its value given on the show? To make this easier, each estimate includes the first initial of the person or entity that is clued.

Objects:

A fretless guitar owned by **the lead guitarist of an iconic four-piece rock and roll band**

A gold mourning ring containing a lock of hair from **the author of** *Jane Eyre*

A jade, diamond and gold pear blossom branch created by **a Russian enamellist famous for creating intricate eggs**

A prop helmet from the set of **a sci-fi film series created by George Lucas**

A small notebook containing handwritten contemporary reviews of **a prolific Elizabethan playwright**

Signed first editions of children's books featuring animal characters by **a female author with Lake District connections**

Estimated upper values:

£20,000 (C)	**£25,000** (B)	**£30,000** (W)
£50,000 (S)	**£400,000** (G)	**£1,000,000** (F)

LOCATION, LOCATION

Can you identify the recording sites of *Antiques Roadshow* given below? Each location includes CASTLE in its name, but has been changed to remove all of the letters of the word 'CASTLE', wherever they are found in the name. For example, DOVER CASTLE would have been written as DOVR. The county or region of each location is given.

BOOVR (Derbyshire)
BRNRD (County Durham)
HOWRD (North Yorkshire)
HVR (Kent)
KND (Cumbria)
NWIK (Northumberland)
PMBROK (Wales)
RDIFF (Wales)
UKND (County Durham)

THE SKY AT NIGHT

On 4 October 1957, the USSR began the space race with the United States by launching into Earth's orbit Sputnik 1, the first artificial satellite. Around the same time, German astronomer Wilhelm Gliese published the 'Gliese Catalogue of Nearby Stars', identifying 915 known stars within 20 parsecs of Earth.

The monthly programme, which aired late at night, opened and closed to Jean Sibelius' 'At the Castle Gate'. Moore first welcomed audiences on 24 April 1957. His final broadcast was posthumously aired on 7 January 2013, following his death on 9 December 2012. Since 2000, Chris Lintott had been an increasingly regular guest, eventually co-presenting as Moore's health deteriorated. He then co-presented the show with Lucie Green in 2013 and then with Maggie Aderin-Pocock since 2014. The show aired on BBC One until late 2013 when it was moved to BBC Four.

The show's format has remained consistent, highlighting events currently happening in the night sky, major news impacting the scientific field and focusing on space or space-travel related topics. Guests included some of the great luminaries of the scientific and astronomical world of the 20th and 21st century. But for 55 years, the show was driven by the passion and knowledge of Moore.

Universal interest in what lay outside our atmosphere was growing, so the BBC's decision to commission a programme some six months earlier that looked at what lay above us in the heavens was more than a little timely. What was not known was how popular among a select audience *The Sky at Night* would remain, transforming amateur astronomer Patrick Moore into a beloved figure of British broadcasting. And his tenure as host made *The Sky at Night* the longest-running programme with the same presenter in television history.

Patrick Moore (right); Moore pictured with Queen guitarist and songwriter Brian May, himself an astrophysicist (above).

THE NATURAL ORDER

How good is your astronomical knowledge? Can you label these historical events in chronological order, from earliest (1) to most recent (10)?

___ Apollo 11 astronauts are the first to walk on the moon

___ Curiosity rover lands on Mars

___ Edmond Halley first predicts the appearance of the periodical comet

___ First long-term residents arrive at the International Space Station

___ Hubble Space Telescope launched

___ NASA founded

___ Pluto reclassified as a dwarf planet

___ Royal Observatory, Greenwich, founded

___ Sputnik 1 is launched by the USSR

___ The planet Uranus is discovered

OBSCURED OBJECTS

Each of the astronomical objects below has been disguised by changing exactly one letter in its name. Can you identify all of the hidden celestial items? The incorrect letters spell out, in the order given, the name of a figure linked to *The Sky at Night*.

SUM

BLOCK HOLE

OARS

COMER

VENUE

ASTRONOMY QUIZ

Can you use your knowledge of the night sky to answer the following questions? The solutions are listed beneath, but are given out of order – and every other letter is missing.

1. Which is the only planet in the solar system to be named after a god from Greek mythology?
2. Which is the brightest star in the night sky?
3. What type of celestial body, found in our solar system, is Ceres?
4. What is the Latin name for the North Star?
5. Who was Britain's first astronaut?

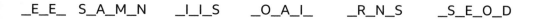

_E_E_ S_A_M_N ___I_I_S ___O_A_I_ ___R_N_S ___S_E_O_D

HORIZON

Have you pondered over the origins of Stonehenge, considered why a cow might make us mad, thought about the origins of the universe, or the composition of the planets? If you have, then there's a strong chance you will have been one of the regular viewers of *Horizon*, a documentary series comprising mostly one-off investigations into the worlds of science, nature, philosophy and an ephemera so wide, one of the pleasures of watching the programme was to discover where each episode would take us.

The BBC Two programme first aired on 2 May 1964, a month after the station was launched. In structure, it took its cue from the popular arts magazine programme *Monitor*, which had been on air since 1958. It even had its own mission statement: 'to provide a platform from which some of the world's greatest scientists and philosophers can communicate their curiosity, observations and reflections, and infuse into our common knowledge their changing views of the universe'. The first episode presented a profile of polymath Richard Buckminster Fuller, perfectly encapsulating the series' desire to balance an exploration of science in every form with the people involved in it.

The show was a team effort, written mostly in-house by the production team and advisers, with the presenter appearing – for the most part – off-screen. Still running strong, *Horizon* has broadcast more than 1,250 episodes. The tone of the series has lightened since the early 2000s and occasionally been fronted by well-known figures, but it still tackles a wide range of topics, from issues surrounding drone technology and the debate around e-cigarettes to the workings of CERN and the coronavirus.

One-time presenter Dan Wallace (above) and regular show hosts Michael Mosley and Hannah Fry (right).

A QUESTION OF QUESTIONS

Each of the questions below – when complete – is the name of an episode of *Horizon*. The crucial words needed to finish the titles have been removed, however, and placed into the wordsearch grid below. The number of letters in each missing word is given to help you, and the words in the grid may be written in any direction, including diagonally. Can you complete all of the titles?

1. Are We Alone in the _____ (8)?
2. Are We Still _____ (8)?
3. Can _____ (6) Survive?
4. Can We Make a _____ (4) on Earth?
5. Could _____ (4) Make My Child Smart?
6. Did _____ (7) Make Us Human?
7. Did _____ (6) Get It Wrong?
8. Do _____ (4) Make You Mad?
9. Do We Really Need the _____ (8)?
10. Do You Dig National _____ (5)?
11. How Long is a Piece of _____ (6)?
12. How Much Do You _____ (5)?
13. How Safe is _____ (7)?
14. Should We Close Our _____ (4)?
15. So You Want to Be an _____ (8)?
16. What Makes an _____ (6) Smart?
17. What Really Killed the _____ (9)?
18. What's Killing Our _____ (4)?
19. What's Wrong with the _____ (3)?
20. Where Must the _____ (5) Go?
21. Who Will Deliver Your _____ (4)?

S	R	Z	O	I	O	O	I	I	O	Z	O	O	H	O
T	O	Y	Z	O	D	Y	R	E	G	R	U	S	O	H
R	Z	R	E	U	I	S	E	E	B	N	O	N	I	O
I	O	H	R	N	N	O	H	I	H	N	L	I	O	H
N	R	N	E	I	O	Z	Z	N	G	R	A	T	S	O
G	R	O	V	V	S	M	R	V	N	R	M	R	N	O
E	N	R	I	E	A	R	H	E	I	H	I	N	Z	N
C	O	A	L	R	U	O	I	N	K	S	N	I	I	H
I	Z	I	E	S	R	H	U	T	O	K	A	W	I	R
N	I	L	D	E	S	S	N	O	O	R	R	I	O	R
E	I	W	H	I	O	M	N	R	C	A	H	N	C	I
V	O	A	F	N	R	H	E	R	D	P	S	O	I	O
O	I	Y	Z	O	O	R	O	L	O	I	W	O	N	O
O	Z	S	N	R	N	R	I	I	L	S	O	Z	O	H
Z	R	I	O	Z	R	G	N	I	V	L	O	V	E	Z

THE OPEN UNIVERSITY

With its ambitious aim to increase the size of the university-educated population, the Open University first broadcast on BBC Two on 3 January 1971. Television and radio were the perfect platforms to reach a wide audience. But what soon became apparent was that viewers and listeners beyond the students were tuning in to whatever subject interested them.

The Open University was conceived under Prime Minister Harold Wilson and driven by Minister of State for Education Jennie Lee. Assistant Editor of Engineering James Redmond, who gained his education through night school, overcame technical difficulties to bring the various lecture series on air, with broadcasting taking place at the BBC's recently vacated studios at Alexandra Palace in north London.

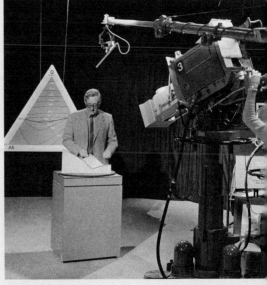

Opening with its iconic logo – a moon-shaped O set within a sky-blue U – and accompanied by Leonard Salzedo's 'Divertimento for Three Trumpets and Three Trombones', the Open University soon proved an effective platform for teaching. Provided, of course, that its audience had the stamina to sustain themselves through its irregular, frequently nocturnal schedule.

Before the emergence of VHS, DVD and the Internet, lectures were slotted in around BBC Two's conventional programming. This meant that any spare hour was available to the OU, but outside peak hours. Courses also rarely changed their lecture programme, so some lecturers' fashions appeared far behind the times. The result was rich terrain for comedians and satirists, who regularly lampooned the style of the programmes. But the Open University's popularity on the BBC during its first decades cemented the foundations of its success.

Open University lecturers frequently had little on-screen training, and so often appeared slightly awkward on screen (left and above).

IRREGULAR PROGRAMMING

Place each of these subject-specific words into the table once each, so that they are listed under a relevant category. Some of the words could fit in multiple columns, but there is only one way to place all of the words simultaneously.

Anther
Area
Circumference
Digit
Hand
Hercules
Iris
Neck

Palm
Percentage
Petal
Root
Sepal
Stamen
Venus
Zeus

Maths Terms	Plant Parts	Body Parts	Greek Myth

HONORARY GRADUATES

Each of these famous faces is an honorary graduate of the Open University. Can you name each person, and match them with the factual BBC programme listed that they have presented or appeared in?

- *Blue Planet II*
- *Julius Caesar Revealed*
- *The Drawing of My Life*
- *University Challenge*

1

2

3

4

DESERT ISLAND DISCS

Opening to the relaxing strains of composer Eric Coates' 'By the Sleepy Lagoon', *Desert Island Discs* has remained a mainstay of British radio and popular culture for 80 years. It is second only to the 'Grand Ole Opry' in the United States as the longest-running radio programme in the world.

A simple but remarkably effective interview format, the show imagines its guest on a desert island. They talk about their life as they name their eight chosen music tracks. At the end, they are accompanied on the island by a religious text, the works of William Shakespeare, a book and a 'luxury' of their choice, along with their favourite of the eight tracks.

The show was devised by Roy Plomley in 1941 after he and his wife were forced to return to England from France following the invasion of the German army. His first guest was actor and radio comedian Vic Oliver, and the show aired on 19 January 1942. Originally running for eight weekly shows, its popularity saw the BBC commission a further 15 shows.

In total, Plomley presented 1,791 editions before leaving the show in 1985. He was succeeded by Michael Parkinson, who hosted until 1988 before Sue Lawley took over and remained as host until 2006. She was replaced by Kirsty Young, who remained until 2018, when Lauren Laverne took over.

The addition of a choice of luxury and books was introduced in 1952, followed by a favourite track in 1959. By the time the show reached its 80th anniversary in 2022, it had aired more than 3,250 episodes.

Boxer Nicola Adams with Kirsty Young (left) and Paul McCartney (right), whose favourite disc was John Lennon's 'Beautiful Boy'.

FREQUENT CASTAWAY

Can you crack the number code and reveal the name of a guest who has appeared on *Desert Island Discs* a surprising four times? No other guest has appeared more often, although this is a record which they share with actor-comedian Arthur Askey.

Solve the crossword clues given opposite, filling in the solutions from left to right with one letter per box. Each solution box has been labelled with a number, with the same number replacing the same letter across the entire puzzle.

The fifth and sixth lines – shaded here – reveal the name of the guest, and can be completed by working out the letter associated with each number.

Clever

2	9	5	8	11	12

Inspiring of affection

1	3	4	1	7	9	5	3	8

Held dear

7	4	13	9	1	4

One who explores

7	4	10	1	3	12	6	9	1	9

4	7	10	5	4

7	12	12	1	3	2	13	9	13	6	8	11

PLAY IT AGAIN

The names of ten songs, all by the artist or group most frequently chosen by castaways on *Desert Island Discs*, have been clued below in rather literal ways. Can you solve all ten clues and reveal the names of the ten pieces of music? Who is the artist or group? The lengths of the words in each clued song title are given in brackets after each clue.

Gather (4, 8)
Our closest star is arriving (4, 5, 3, 3)
Allow it to exist (3, 2, 2)
Only feelings of adoration are required (3, 3, 4, 2, 4)
Turdus merula (9)
During the soft lachrymation of my six-stringed instrument (5, 2, 6, 6, 5)
Alongside small amounts of assistance from my companions (4, 1, 6, 4, 4, 2, 7)
Rotate and yell (5, 3, 5)
Pastures of red, seeded fruits indefinitely (10, 6, 7)
The day immediately preceding today (9)

WOMAN'S HOUR

One of the longest-running and most popular magazine shows on BBC Radio, *Woman's Hour* has become an essential part of the BBC's output. Always intended to talk directly to a female audience about their everyday lives and the issues they face, over the years it has challenged the status quo when it comes to the role of women in society and proven remarkably resilient in the face of criticism.

Presented by Alan Ivimey when it first aired on 7 October 1946, the show's creation is credited to producer Norman Collins. However, Janet Quigley, who also originated the *Today* programme, is acknowledged as a driving force behind it. Ivimey was joined by Mary Hill, who remained on the show until 1963. Over the years, it has featured long-standing hosts, most notably Sue MacGregor (1972–87), Jenni Murray (1987–2020) and Jane Garvey (2007–20). Following Murray and Garvey's departure, Emma Barnett and Anita Rani were appointed as the show's permanent hosts.

Initially airing at 2pm on weekday afternoons, in 1991 *Woman's Hour* was moved to 10.30am, before finding its current home at 10am. *Weekend Woman's Hour*, which offers highlights of the week, is broadcast at 4pm on Saturdays. The format of the programme has changed over the years. Although it has grappled with important issues, topics have become increasingly less whimsical and segments such as the book review section have a stronger female focus. It has also become less structured and more informal in its style. With the advent of the podcast, the show is also one of the BBC's most popular radio programmes.

Past presenters Jean Metcalfe, M. Anderson and Margaret Hubble (above), Jenni Murray and Jane Garvey with Lauren Laverne (right).

THE FIRST HOURS

At 2pm on 7 October 1946, the first-ever *Woman's Hour* was broadcast. One of the early producers to work on the show, Diana Grayford, gave an interview to Emma Barnett on the 75th birthday of *Woman's Hour* in 2021, in which she described the four 'domestic' topics that made up most of the first shows. These four topics are listed below, but they have had any letters also found in 'HOUR' removed. Can you work out what the topics are?

1. CKEY

2. AIDESSING

3. CILDCAE

4. FASIN

Once you have identified the topics, see if you can also guess what the following quote from Diana Grayford originally said, before every second letter was removed:

'B_l_e_e t_a_ w_m_n _r_ i_t_r_se_ i_ e_e_y_h_n_ – a_s_l_t_l e_e_y_h_n_'

FACES ON THE RADIO

Can you identify each of these women who has each served as a guest editor on *Woman's Hour*? Their names are listed, although all the letters in each name have been anagrammed into alphabetical order.

1. ACEEIJLNQU ILNOSW

2. ADEM EKLLY EHLMOS

3. AEWZ AHNOST

4. EEILL DIMMNOSS

5. IKM AACLLRTT

6. J K GILNORW

TOMORROW'S WORLD

What will our world look like in the coming decades? How will science and technology improve or change our lives? These were just two of the questions that this magazine-format programme grappled with as it introduced and explored a world of invention and innovation. By turns inspiring and whimsical, *Tomorrow's World* presented a mostly optimistic take on what humanity could achieve.

The series was created in 1965 by producer Glyn Jones, who was asked by the BBC to fill six 30-minute weekly slots over the summer. He had previously presented *Challenge*, television's first science magazine programme, which presented an annual overview of recent technological achievements. (He would also go on to create *Horizon*.) The name for the new show was devised by Jones and his wife the night before the *Radio Times* went to press.

Tomorrow's World presenters of the past: Raymond Baxter (top left) and Peter Snow and Philippa Forrester (right).

The show was initially presented by Raymond Baxter, with the first episode looking at kidney dialysis, flood defences and the possibility of uncovering life on Mars. It was presented live, which occasionally resulted in the failure of certain inventions to perform to their optimum.

But more notable was first-look introduction to items that would become commonplace in everyday life, from the home computer (1967), pocket calculator (1971) and digital watch (1972) to the mobile phone (1979), compact disc player (1981) and wind-up radio (1994). The show also covered innovations in industry and medicine, such as targeted intra-operative radiotherapy for breast cancer (2000).

Although the show has not had a regular presence on air since 2003, with its live in-studio demonstrations replaced by pre-recorded items in the mid-1990s, *Tomorrow's World* has enjoyed occasional one-off programmes, most recently with a show presented in 2018.

THEY NEED NO INTRODUCTION

The following inventions or techniques showcased on *Tomorrow's World* have now become familiar concepts and objects and need no further introduction. With that in mind, their 'introductions' have been removed – that is, their first letter has been deleted, both at the start of their first word and also anywhere else that same letter appears within the invention. For example, COMPACT DISC would have become OMPAT DIS, with the initial 'C' removed three times. Can you reveal all eight incredible inventions?

- RTIFICIL GRSS
- LCTRONIC VIDO RCORDR
- N VTRO FERTLZATON
- ONORDE
- ELEEX
- YNTHEIZER
- AMORDER
- ERIL MPPING

FUTURE FINDINGS

Hidden in the puzzle below are references to some of the more unusual features on *Tomorrow's World*. Each entry clues a word that can be found in the grid by moving horizontally or vertically between letters, spelling out the solutions as you go. Start at the arrow and finish at the star, but note the clues are not given in the same order as they are found in the path.

- **Glow-in-the-dark equipment for what sport was featured on the show?**
- **Hissing Sid was a robot that could supposedly play which sport?**
- **What material did the show predict that underwear, suits and dresses would be made from in the future?**
- **What was the name of the robotic housemaid that featured on the show in 1966?**
- **Which common mode of transport was shown with inflatable attachments to allow it to ride on water?**
- **Which German electronic band played live on the show in 1975, marking their first British TV appearance?**
- **Worms were touted as a source of future protein. What food were they eaten in on the show?**

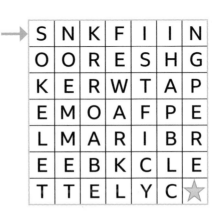

SIR DAVID ATTENBOROUGH

A towering figure of British broadcasting, Sir David Attenborough has used his considerable influence to popularize natural history programming and, in more recent years, the threat we pose to the environment.

Developing an affinity for nature as a child, Attenborough studied geology and zoology at Clare College, Cambridge. After national service and a brief period editing children's science textbooks, Attenborough took a job as a producer at the BBC. Soon after, he produced and presented the natural history programme *Animal Patterns* (1953), followed by the series *Zoo Quest* (1954–59).

In 1965, Attenborough became Controller of BBC Two. Under his tenure, having previously lacked an identity, the channel became bold in its vision. He was responsible for commissioning *Call My Bluff* (1965), *Civilisation* (1969), *Monty Python's Flying Circus* (1969), *The Old Grey Whistle Test* (1971) and *The Ascent of Man* (1973). Nature came calling again, and in 1976 he began three years of research and filming for the first of his epic natural history documentary series: *Life on Earth* (1979). It broke new ground in terms of technological innovation and involved 1.5 million miles of travel to record life on the planet, including Attenborough's now legendary encounter with mountain gorillas in Rwanda.

The various *Life* series, along with the two series of *The Blue Planet* and his many one-off documentaries, have made Attenborough one of the most respected and popular science presenters in television history and a national treasure in his home country.

A beloved figure, Attenborough's instantly recognizable voice has been a familiar sound on the BBC for more than five decades.

HIDDEN WILDLIFE

Can you spot the well-disguised wildlife hidden in each of the following sentences? There is one animal per line, each with a name consisting of six or more letters. For example, 'monkey' has been hidden in 'I'm on keynote speaker lists for a few wildlife organizations'.

1. We'll either get to the safari camp by driving, or I'll arrange a helicopter flight.

2. Did he say bring a cap, or cup? I never know what to bring on these expeditions.

3. Where did you send the camera operator to? I searched high and low but they're not on set.

4. It would cause absolute havoc to push the filming schedule into hurricane season!

WHAT'S IN A NAME?

David Attenborough has been honoured by having several species of animal and flower named after him. Many of these are rare – and one is extinct. Six of these eponymous animals have their Latin name given below. Can you complete the English name of each critter, by using two or more of the provided word fragments to complete each gap? The number of letters in each missing word is given to help you, and each word fragment is used exactly once.

1. *Zaglossus attenboroughi* – long-beaked _____ (7)

2. *Pristimantis attenboroughi* – Attenborough's rubber _____ (4)

3. *Platysaurus attenboroughi* – Attenborough's flat _____ (6)

4. *Electrotettix attenboroughi* – pygmy _____ (6)

5. *Attenborosaurus conybeari* – marine _____ (7)

6. *Trigonopterus attenboroughii* – flightless _____ (6)

EC	EV	FR	HID
IL	LE	LI	LOC
NA	OG	PTI	RD
RE	UST	WE	ZA

Children's Television

For anyone born since the 1960s, their childhood memories
will include a favourite television programme or two. *Watch
with Mother* began in the 1950s, but by the 1960s, children's
television programming had widened significantly. While studio
programmes such as the long-standing *Blue Peter* offered a
variation on adult's magazine programmes, other shows created
magical, mythic and alien worlds. From *Bill and Ben* to *Trumpton*,
Andy Pandy to *Shaun the Sheep* and *Mr Benn* to *Postman Pat*
and *Pingu*, children's television revelled in the wondrous. And
through programmes like *Grange Hill* and *Byker Grove* it also
engaged older audiences in the realities of everyday life. Some
shows transcended their age group and the era in which they
were made. If *Bagpuss* conjured up a strange past and *The Magic
Roundabout* gave us a trippy alternate reality, *Teletubbies* created
an entertainment for the very young that remains as strange and
alluring today as the first time it was aired.

EARLY CHILDREN'S TV

Children's programming was an early feature of the BBC's television broadcasting. *For the Children*, a ten-minute programme aimed at a wide age range, was launched on 24 April 1937. It came off-air in 1939 with the outbreak of the Second World War but returned on Sundays in 1946, introducing the popular Muffin the Mule. It was accompanied by the first programme aimed at pre-school children, *For the Very Young*. From then on, children's programmes became a staple of daytime broadcasting.

In 1952, these earlier programmes were replaced by individual programmes for older children and a variety of activities aimed at pre-schoolers that came under the banner *Watch with Mother*. Producers Freda Lingstrom and Maria Bird created a cycle of programmes within this strand that became iconic in the history of children's television, from *Andy Pandy* (from 1950) and *Flower Pot Men* (from 1952) to *The Woodentops* (from 1955), *Camberwick Green* (1966) and *Fingerbobs* (1972). With the launch of BBC Two in 1964, *Play School* was added to the roster of children's programming. It was joined in 1971 by *Play Away*.

Watch with Mother was cancelled in 1975 and replaced in 1980 by *See-Saw*. It's most famous show was *Postman Pat*. In 1985 children's programming was rebranded and came under the remit of Children's BBC. And with it the voiceover was replaced by an on-camera host, the first being Phillip Schofield. In 2002, two new dedicated digital channels were created for children: CBBC for children aged six to thirteen, and CBeebies for pre-schoolers.

Annette Mills with Muffin the Mule (left); Pat Keysell and Tony Hart, presenters of *Vision On*, a programme for deaf children (right).

WATCH WITH MOTHER

Five of the shows that featured on *Watch with Mother* were each played on a different weekday as part of a regular cycle. Can you use the clues below to work out which shows were played on which days from 1955 onwards?

- *Picture Book* was shown earlier in the week than *Flower Pot Men*
- *Rag, Tag and Bobtail* was not the programme shown on Fridays
- *Andy Pandy* was shown earlier in the week than *The Woodentops*
- *Flower Pot Men* was shown on Wednesdays
- *Rag, Tag and Bobtail* was shown later in the week than *Andy Pandy*
- *Picture Book* was not shown on Tuesdays

Monday: _____

Tuesday: _____

Wednesday: _____

Thursday: _____

Friday: _____

MUFFIN THE MULE

First appearing on *For the Children* in 1946, the puppet Muffin the Mule was joined in later episodes by several animal friends. Each of the animals had names whose first letter was shared with the type of animal they were, just as 'Muffin' and 'Mule' share the initial 'M'.

Can you work out what type of animal each of these characters was, writing in one letter per underline below? The type of animal is given to help you, along with one of the letters.

1. Kirri the _ _ _ I   (bird)
2. Zebbie the _ _ _ R _   (mammal)
3. Hubert the _ _ _ P _ _ _ _ _ _ _ _   (mammal)
4. Sally the _ _ _ L   (mammal)
5. Grace the _ _ _ _ F _ _   (mammal)
6. Oswald the _ S _ _ _ _ _   (bird)
7. Peregrine the _ _ _ G _ _ _   (bird)

ALL-TIME FAVOURITES

In more than 75 years, the BBC has produced a plethora of memorable children's programmes. Outside screenings of international shows, ranging from *Champion the Wonder Horse* and *Lassie* and dubbed versions of European dramas such as *The Flashing Blade* and *Heidi*, the BBC produced an extraordinary number of programmes with huge appeal.

or of alternate realities and fantasy lands. They ranged from some of the earliest programmes, from *Andy Pandy* (1950) and *Flower Pot Men* (1952) through to the trippy *The Magic Roundabout* (1965), the pastoral *Postman Pat* (1981), a chilly *Pingu* (1990) and those perennial favourites *Teletubbies* (1997).

The Wombles (1973) created an entire world beneath London's Wimbledon Common, while *Clangers* (1969) enjoyed life on the moon. *Mr Benn* (1971–72) took off on adventures around the world, and *Bagpuss* (1974) found them at home. And while various incarnations of Doctor Who have terrified young audiences across a lifetime that spans 60 years and counting, it helped define their memories of television.

While the long-running *Grange Hill* (1978–2008) and *Byker Grove* (1989–2006) reflected the lives of British teenagers, other shows sought to inspire, as *Blue Peter* has done since first airing in 1958 and *Record Breakers* (1972–2001) did in its long run. Still others were merely happy to indulge in a bout of chaos, whether in the past of *Horrible Histories* (from 2009) or the mania of the popular children's competitive show *Crackerjack!*, which began in 1955 and was recommissioned in 2020.

For many, their most nostalgic memories are of the shows they watched when they were very young, filled with a sense of wonder at the world

Michael Aspel, host of *Crackerjack* from 1968–74 (left); Alan Bennett reading *The House at Pooh Corner* for *Jackanory* in 1996 (right).

SOUND AND VISION

Each of these theme-tune lyrics can be completed by filling in the title of the children's show it comes from. To help you, pictured below are stills from each of these programmes. Can you fill in the gaps, and match each lyric to its image?

1. '_____ and his black and white cat'

2. '_____ of Wimbledon Common are we'

3. 'There's so much to see, so _____'

4. 'Bill and Ben _____'

5. 'He's always on the scene: _____ _____ !'

6. 'What's the story in _____, wouldn't you like to know?'

THE MAGIC ROUNDABOUT

From its unique genesis to the significant following it attracted beyond its core young audience, *The Magic Roundabout* occupies a singular presence on the landscape of children's television. Created by Serge Danot, then reinvented for an English audience by Eric Thompson, in its iteration for the BBC the show is a colourful phantasmagoria that delighted the young while tapping into the zeitgeist of the late 1960s counterculture.

Having first aired in France in 1964, the BBC originally turned it down, seeing the translation of the scripts as an onerous task. But actor and director Eric Thompson, who was a presenter on *Play School* from 1964–67, convinced the broadcaster to purchase the series on the proviso that he would rewrite the scripts. With no knowledge of the original storylines,

Thompson created a series of playful episodes, populated by a collection of strange creatures that included the dog Dougal, snail Brian, cow Ermintrude and hippy rabbit, all of whom were residents of The Magic Garden. There were also the humans Florence and Mr Rusty, the roundabout operator, and Zebedee, a magical jack-in-the-box.

The first series was shot in black and white, and a colour episode was not screened on British television until October 1970. Each episode lasted just five minutes and aired directly before the early evening news every weekday. Danot also made a film in 1970, which Thompson adapted in 1972. *Dougal and the Blue Cat* pushed the trippy vibe of the series even further and became a cult favourite, watched as much by adults as children.

Florence and Dougal amid the paper flowers of The Magic Garden.

SPIN THE CAROUSEL

Can you work out how you could rotate the rings below so that all of the answers to the following questions can be read simultaneously, reading outwards from the centre of the circle?

- How many millions of viewers watched *The Magic Roundabout* at its peak?
- What was the name of the rabbit character, taken from that of a famous countercultural musician?
- What type of creature was the character named 'Ambroise' in the original French version? It was named 'Brian' in the BBC show.
- What kind of unusual abilities did the jack-in-the-box character possess?
- How many wheels were on the vehicle ridden by the elderly gardener?
- What type of musical instrument features heavily in the theme tune?

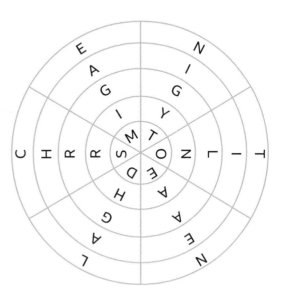

IN A ROUNDABOUT WAY

The titular *Magic Roundabout* was located an unspecified distance from 'The Magic Garden', where all of the characters in the programme lived. Indeed, some of the characters even teleported between the two locations, so the route was never revealed. But perhaps you can find your own?

Draw a single loop that visits every white square in the grid opposite exactly once each, plus also visits the Magic Garden (marked with a green square) and the Magic Roundabout (marked with a yellow square). The loop can't enter any of the black squares.

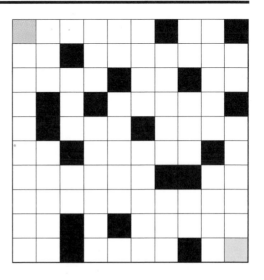

BAGPUSS

First aired in 1974, *Bagpuss* opens with a series of sepia images of a world gone by, while narrator Oliver Postgate informs us that 'Once upon a time. Not so long ago. There was a little girl. And her name was Emily. And she had a shop.' Across 13 episodes, Postgate and illustrator Peter Firmin's magical stop-motion animation brought wonder into its young viewers' worlds.

Through still images, Emily (Firmin's daughter) is seen bringing a broken object to her shop and whispering magical words into the ear of the titular 'saggy old cloth cat': 'Bagpuss, dear Bagpuss / fat, furry catpuss / wake up and look at this thing that I bring / wake up, be bright, be golden and light / Bagpuss, oh hear what I sing'. And with those words, the cat comes to life – a benevolent pink-and-white-striped creature. No sooner has he stretched than the mice on the mouse organ, the ragdoll Madeleine, banjo-playing toad Gabriel and Professor Yaffle, a woodpecker bookend come to life. Each episode, the characters work to fix the object Emily brought them and then return to being inanimate objects. Madeleine conjures a story from the object and Gabriel sings a song about it, encouraging children to let their imaginations run free.

Postgate supplied all voices, save for Madeleine and Gabriel, who were voiced by folk musicians Sandra Kerr and John Faulkner, who also composed the show's wistful music. Quite unlike anything else, *Bagpuss* would become one of the most beloved of children's programmes.

Legendary children's storyteller Oliver Postgate (above); Madeleine, the ragdoll, Gabriel the singing toad and one of the mice (right).

LOST AND FOUND

All but one of the items listed below were seen in Emily's shop window on *Bagpuss*, meaning that somebody had lost them. Find these items in the wordsearch grid, and in so doing identify the missing item. It is an item that, in one episode of the show, the characters expected to find in the shop window but did not. For a bonus, what tricked them into thinking that the absent item existed?

BALLET SHOE
BASKET
BROKEN FIGURINE
CUSHION COVER
LEPRECHAUN

LOOM
OLD BUCKET
RAGDOLL HOUSE
SELF-PLAYING FIDDLE
SHIP IN A BOTTLE

STATUETTE
STRAW ELEPHANT
TANGLED PLANT
TOY MILL
TWIG BROOM

BAGPUSS & Co

```
L B S G L M G T Z G A U O N S J D
L R E V O C N O I H S U C B E M I
U O E O I A T Y V W Q Y L L L O Q
X K L J R F Z M T B T V E T F O F
L E T D C J C I N O Y C F S P R W
L N T T B M H L A X Q S T C L B G
I F O U P U N L L X H A R Y A G W
A I B U W K C K P M T B K G Y I Y
U G A H Z E D K D U A K T L I W S
X U N S T R A W E L E P H A N T C
G R I D U O G T L T E L P Q G M H
A I P D A V T E G Q U Q W O F O O
X N I P J E T X N D S G G U I O X
I E H Q G S G B A S K E T D D M A
Z J S Z H F O P T G S Z P A D U Q
X Q A O F K O F Y G G H E B L W V
B P E R A G D O L L H O U S E L P
```

LITTLE MYSTERIES

See if you can answer the following questions about the programme *Bagpuss*. The solutions are given beneath to help you, but the letters have been jumbled up – and they are in a different order.

1. **Which British philosopher was the wooden woodpecker Professor Yaffle based on?**
2. **In which Kent city does the real cloth Bagpuss currently reside?**
3. **Which Greek city is claimed by the toys to be the home of the owls on the decorative cushion cover?**
4. **What colour were Bagpuss's stripes originally supposed to be, but came out pink after a manufacturing error?**
5. **The frog Gabriel was named after a character in which long-running BBC radio drama?**

- **AN OGRE**
- **HASTEN**
- **CHARTS HERE**

- **CENTURY BAR**
- **BLURRED 'N' ARTLESS**

BLUE PETER

The longest-running children's television show in the world, *Blue Peter* was conceived as a magazine-style programme for younger audiences. Over the course of 62 years, it has become something of a national institution and one of the BBC's best-loved shows.

Devised by John Hunter Blair and aimed at an audience that had outgrown the pre-school programme *Watch with Mother*, which began in 1952, *Blue Peter* first aired on 16 October 1958. It took its name from the flag hoisted when a ship is ready to set sail from port. Combining live broadcast and pre-recorded segments, the show's overarching concept was that each episode would take its viewers on a journey of knowledge and discovery.

The first programme was 15 minutes long and modest in its aims. It became a more significant feature of the BBC's programming schedule with the arrival of Biddy Baxter, a producer and editor who effectively skippered *Blue Peter*'s output from 1962 to her retirement in 1988. She devised the Blue Peter badge in 1963, to encourage viewers to engage with the show by sending in letters, pictures and

John Noakes with Shep.

Konnie Huq, Gethin Jones, Andy Akinwolere and Helen Skelton from the 2000s.

ideas. She also instituted the annual appeals, raising awareness of charities and issues by encouraging novel ways to fundraise.

The show has had 40 presenters across its first 60 years, generally comprising three at any point. The most famous trio, who appeared together in the late 1960s, were Valerie Singleton – who personified the role of the show's roving reporter – Peter Purves and John Noakes, whose pet dog Shep was also a mainstay on the programme.

Presenters during the 1980s: Peter Duncan, Sarah Greene and Simon Groom.

PET NAMES

Listed below are the names of all but one of the *Blue Peter* pets who have appeared on the programme, as of the start of 2022 (including two Barneys!). Enter each name into the empty grid, one letter per box, so one name can be read across each row. The name of the final pet can then be found by jumbling the letters found in the dashed-line boxes.

Green rows are tortoises, blue rows are parrots, orange rows are cats, yellow rows are dogs, and the white row is a pony.

BARNEY	JASON	PATCH
BARNEY	JILL	PETRA
BONNIE	JIM	RAGS
COOKIE	JOEY	SHELLEY
FREDA	KARI	SHEP
GEORGE	MABEL	SMUDGE
GOLDIE	MAGGIE	SOCKS
HENRY	MEG	WILLOW
JACK	OKE	

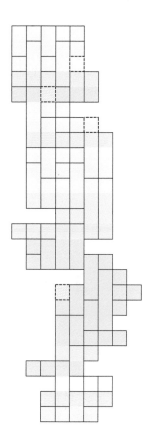

BADGE OF HONOUR

Pictured here are the eight different badges available to *Blue Peter* viewers as of 2022. Can you match each badge to one of the descriptions below?

- Awarded in exceptional circumstances, and only to those with an existing badge, for an outstanding achievement such as saving someone's life
- Awarded to those who join the *Blue Peter* fan club
- Awarded to those who send interesting letters or items for the programme, as well as those who appear on the show
- Awarded to competition winners and runners-up
- Awarded to those who complete pledges to help the environment
- Awarded to those who already have a blue badge, and send in an interesting letter or item

HORRIBLE HISTORIES

Actor, director and author Terry Deary created his *Horrible Histories* book series by chance. A publisher suggested he write a book with jokes interspersed with historical facts. However, as he noted, 'when I looked at the facts, I found they were much more interesting than the jokes. So we ended up with a fact book with jokes. We created a new genre.' *The Terrible Tudors* and *The Awesome Egyptians* were published in 1993 and became a huge success.

Deary worked with writers Peter Hepplewhite and Neil Tonge, alongside illustrators Martin Brown, Philip Reeve and Mike Phillips. In 2001, an animated series was made of the books. But it was the BBC's 2009 live-action series that proved an outstanding success with audiences.

Developed for the CBBC strand, by Dominic Brigstocke and Caroline Norris, *Horrible Histories* ran for five years and comprised five series of 13 half-hour episodes, each hosted by the puppet Rattus Rattus. Like its source, the show presented factually accurate representations of some of British and Western history's more gruesome events, shot through with its signature humour. Featuring a cast best known in the British comedy scene, it drew on *Monty Python*'s absurdism and *Blackadder*'s playfulness while carving its own clear identity and, like the books, attracting a large young audience.

In 2011, CBBC launched a game show inspired by the books, along with a new series, this time with Stephen Fry as host. The success of this series and subsequent re-runs prompted another series to be commissioned in 2015, and they continue to be made.

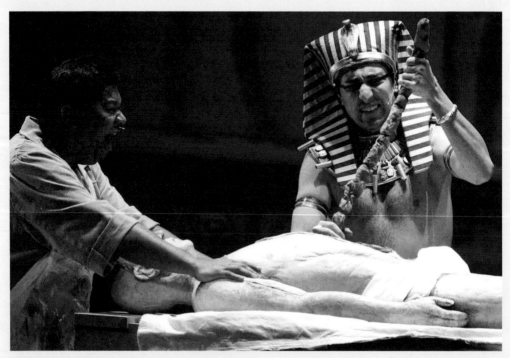

Parodying the ancient Egyptians (above), the Romans and the Tudors, among others, the *Horrible Histories* team also took its tales to the stage.

TERRIFIC TITLES

Distinct periods of history are often introduced in the series with alliterative topic cards that mimic the titles of the original books, such as 'Incredible Incas'. All of the topic cards listed here, however, have been split into two, with a descriptive word on the left and its corresponding historical period on the right. Rather horribly, the names on the right have been anagrammed and are not listed in the same order as the descriptions. Can you unscramble these anagrams and then match up the adjectives to reveal the correct eight names? Note that one of the titles is not alliterative.

If, for example, 'EZ ACTS' appeared on the right then it could be anagrammed to 'AZTECS', then paired with 'Angry' on the left to form 'Angry Aztecs'.

Awful	KEGERS
Gorgeous	NO ARMS
Groovy	ROT SUD
Rotten	SIN TO VICAR
Slimy	SKIVING
Terrible	SORE AGING
Vicious	STRATUS
Vile	TEA SPYING

FAMOUS FIGURES

In many of the sketches featured on *Horrible Histories*, actors play real-life figures from the time periods covered by the show. In the image below, six such historical figures are shown. Their names have also been given next to the image, but without any of their vowels. Using this information, can you work out which six people are depicted in the image, and who is who?

Can you then match five of these revealed figures with an appropriate title card from the previous puzzle?

CHRLS DCKNS

DWRD D VR

JLS CSR

MRY SHLLY

RMSSS

RNST SHCKLTN

CLASSIC ANIMATION

Animation has played a key role in children's programming. Ranging from hand-drawn and stop-motion to more recent innovations in computer-generated imagery, animation has helped define children's interaction with the world around them and also with cultures around the world.

As the number of hours dedicated to children's programming increased, the BBC, like other broadcasters, bought in a variety of international animation series. These ranged from classic cartoons from the United States and studio houses that included Disney and Hanna-Barbera, the latter co-creating the *Tom and Jerry* series before going on to create *Yogi Bear*, *The Flintstones*, *Top Cat*, *Wacky Races* and *Scooby-Doo*.

Animation also lay at the heart of the BBC's domestic production of children's programming and entertainment. *Andy Pandy* was an early example and proved an enormous success. It revolved around the titular marionette and his friends, the teddy bear Teddy and rag doll Looby Loo – who comes to life when the other two aren't around – all of whom live in a picnic basket. It was joined by *Flower Pot Men* and followed by popular stop-motion series such as the Trumptonshire trilogy, comprising *Camberwick Green*, *Trumpton* and *Chigley*.

Stop-motion became a constant over the decades, running the gamut from *The Magic Roundabout*, *Clangers*, *The Wombles* and *Bagpuss* to the early series of *Postman Pat*, *Pingu*, *Bob the Builder* and *Shaun the Sheep*, the latter coming from the creators of Wallace and Gromit. More classical animation took the form of everyman fantasist *Mr Benn*, *Captain Pugwash* and, in more recent years, *Charlie and Lola*.

Children gather around the television to watch an episode of *Andy Pandy*.

ROUND THEM UP

In one episode of *Shaun the Sheep*, Shaun's flock of sheep run away on the bus to a local amusement park, and have to be rounded up again by the sheepdog before the farmer notices. Can you play sheepdog and mark out a loop that travels from the green farm to the red amusement park and back again, visiting every white square along the way? Your route cannot enter any square more than once, nor enter or cross over any black square.

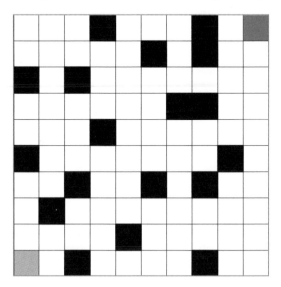

FLOWER POT MEN

Can you work out the name of the turtle from *Flower Pot Men*, based on the letters on the back of the turtle below? It can be reassembled by using each outer letter once, and then the central letter twice. To help you, its name is also a regular English word.

There are also more than 25 other words of three or more letters which can be found on the turtle. For each word, use the centre letter (once) plus any other combination of letters (no more than once per appearance on the turtle). How many can you find?

To get you started, some of the extra words have an animal theme. Here are clues for these:

- **Bovine** (3)
- **Sound a wolf might make** (4)
- **Nocturnal bird** (3)
- **Group of fish** (5)
- **Female pig** (3)

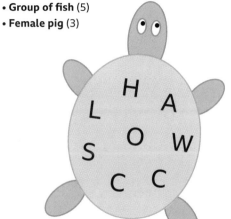

169

TELETUBBIES

Even when compared to some of the more outré examples of children's television programming over the course of its history, this series, about four colourful characters who speak their own unique language and live in a pastoral idyll presided over by an infant sun, is a surreal concoction. The intentionally repetitive adventures of Tinky Winky, Dipsy, Laa-Laa and Po became a sensation with the programme's intended audience, while courting controversy with some parents who felt that their children might start imitating the characters' gibberish.

The Teletubbies live in a home known as the Tubbytronic Superdome, buried beneath a field populated with rabbits. The characters live alongside an array of objects such as the Voice Trumpets and the Noo-Noo, a housekeeping vacuum cleaner. Each episode comprises a series of subtly changing rituals that, like the vibrant colour schemes employed, were designed to engage with young children's attention span and developing minds. A magical event would take place each episode, all watched over by the sun, which features the face of a giggling infant.

The series was created by children's television producers and educators Anne Wood and Andrew Davenport. It first aired on 31 March 1997. By February 2001, when the first version of the show ended, 365 episodes had aired. The show was reprised in 2015 and ran for 120 episodes, before ending on 12 October 2018. Its international success saw it become one of the most lucrative shows in the BBC's history.

Each of the Teletubbies had a TV screen belly on which footage would appear during the show.

TELLING TELETUBBIES TIPS

Can you use the clues below to work out the colour, antenna shape and favourite item of each of the four Teletubbies? Their colours are purple, yellow, green and red.

- **The green Teletubby has a straight antenna**
- **The Teletubby with a spiral antenna loves their orange ball**
- **Po's favourite item is a scooter**
- **Laa-Laa is yellow**
- **The Teletubby with the triangular antenna loves their handbag**
- **Dipsy loves their hat**
- **Po has a circular antenna**
- **Tinky Winky is purple**

THE VOICE TRUMPETS

In the *Teletubbies* revival, several well-known actors took on the spoken roles of 'Voice Trumpets'. They appear at the end of the show and are able to speak in full sentences, but their faces are never seen. The names of five of these actors are given here, but they have been warped into 'voice trumpets' emerging from the ground, just as they do in the show. Can you identify them?

Lifestyle

Lifestyle programmes have changed over the years. When they first began airing, the word 'lifestyle' wasn't even commonly used. Early gardening and cookery programmes better resembled public information films, their hosts more formal in imparting titbits of information about the best way to tend to your garden or make the most of the ingredients in your kitchen. The programmes' functionality reflected the mind-set of a nation less used to leisure than work. But the 1950s saw a gradual change that reflected the way the nation spent their time. Hosts became celebrities and their style of presentation more informal and relaxed. The scope and range of activities increased significantly. Gardening became landscaping and embraced environmental concerns. DIY transformed into home improvement that dealt with every facet of domestic life. And cooking embraced a vast industry of styles and cuisines.

TV CHEFS

Television proved a fertile medium for chefs from all walks of life. And as the British public's taste widened, embracing the cookery from the country's expanding diaspora, so cookery shows branched out to celebrate and indulge in its consuming passions.

Philip Harben paved the way. The UK's first celebrity chef was born into an acting family and ran a popular restaurant in north London until the beginning of the Second World War. An eye injury ended his active service, but his culinary skills were put to use on a radio programme in 1942. By 1946, he was hosting the TV show *Cookery*, which ran for five years.

Harben was succeeded by Fanny Craddock, who became a household name through her television shows from 1955. Her colourful approach to cooking, playing as much on her personality as her skills in the kitchen, would echo through to presenters such as Keith Floyd, a TV chef who is remembered equally for his prodigious consumption of wine as for his flamboyant style.

More sedate, but no less popular, was Delia Smith, a self-taught cook who first appeared on the regional magazine programme *Look East* in the 1970s, but whose series of cookery books would pave the way for later TV chefs such as Rick Stein, who graduated out of Floyd's show to become the resident expert on all things seafood, Jamie Oliver, Anjum Anand, Heston Blumenthal, Ainsley Harriott and Nigella Lawson. Alongside these popular chefs were Ruth Mott, The Hairy Bikers (Dave Myers and Si King) and Two Fat Ladies (Clarissa Dickson Wright and Jennifer Paterson), who presented a distinctive take on British cooking.

Antony Worrall Thompson was the first celebrity chef to host *Saturday Kitchen*, from 2003–06).

THE DELIA EFFECT

Scrambled on each line below is an ingredient or piece of kitchen equipment whose popularity soared after being mentioned on the BBC by Delia Smith. In addition, however, one extra letter has been added to each item.

Can you identify all of the ingredients and equipment? The length of each word in each answer is given. The extra letters, when read in order, will spell out the dish made by Delia's first-ever printed recipe.

1. RARE NECK RIBS (11 – ingredient)

2. GESIG (4 – ingredient)

3. FREEZING BEAN POUR (6, 9 – ingredient)

4. MESS ON PRETZEL (5, 7 – equipment)

5. ANTELOPES MEET (8, 4 – equipment)

6. SPURNER (6 – ingredient)

7. SEW PERKS (7 – equipment)

8. BOSS CUT CAKE (5, 5 – ingredient)

9. EATS LAST (3, 3 – ingredient)

10. A HERB BUR (7 – ingredient)

THREE-PART RECIPE

The six chefs listed on the left below have each presented or taken part in BBC shows that each have a three-word name. Can you reassemble each show title, by taking words in order from each column, and then assign them to the appropriate chef? The columns are each given in alphabetical order.

Chef:	Word 1:	Word 2:	Word 3:
Ainsley Harriott	Cook	Bake	Chef
James Martin	Far	Eat	Cook
Jamie Oliver	Junior	Fast	Flavours
Keith Floyd	Nadiya's	Flung	Floyd
Nadiya Hussain	Ready	Naked	Off
Nigella Lawson	The	Steady	Repeat

SATURDAY KITCHEN

In an age when competition-themed cooking and home-improvement shows were attracting sizeable audiences, an easy-going Saturday morning magazine show was created that drew on the BBC's cookery show past while offering an often-humorous commentary on it, as well as relishing in more contemporary culinary tastes.

Saturday Kitchen is such a simple yet tantalizing concept. It began with a pilot hosted by popular chef Ainsley Harriott in 2001, before launching as a BBC production for the Open University from 26 January 2002. The show's host was the relatively unknown Gregg Wallace, who brought to it a cheeky charm and passion for all things food-related. Each week he introduced a guest chef, who would work their way through a variety of recipes, which were interspersed by episodes from archive cookery programmes hosted by the likes of Keith Floyd and Rick Stein.

The show proved a success with audiences, and from the second series it was broadcast live. The third series saw celebrity chef Antony Worrall Thompson take over as host, with the more educational element of the first two series replaced by a lighter entertainment tone. James Martin took over from Thompson in 2006 and remained until 2016. During that time, the show featured spin-off series such as *Spring Kitchen*, *Christmas Kitchen* and the compilation series *Saturday Kitchen: Best Bites*. Throughout, the shows have kept to the original remit of balancing the contemporary with the past and showing how both cooking and eating habits have changed over the years.

'Cheeky chappy' Gregg Wallace (left); legendary Swiss chef and restaurateur Anton Mosimann (right).

A GOOD FIT

Twenty-five notable *Saturday Kitchen* guests are listed below, except that their surnames have been changed into crossword-style clues. Can you identify all of their surnames, then fit them into the grid, crossword-style?

- **Anna** resident of 11 Downing Street (10)
- **Ashley** guitar with a round soundbox (5)
- **Bill** outer castle wall (6)
- **Danny** person who makes flour (6)
- **Dawn** Parisian's nationality (6)
- **Ed** wager (6)
- **Fearne** soft clothing fabric (6)
- **Grace** slight hollow made by an impact (4)
- **Gregory** hotel baggage assistant (6)
- **Helen** someone who makes hand coverings (6)
- **Jay** knife edges (6)
- **Jessie** pottery type; item for sale (4)
- **Jim** valley, especially in the North (4)
- **Jo** company identifier (5)
- **Levison** small forest (4)
- **Mica** home of the Louvre (5)
- **Michael** sporting sphere (4)
- **Naughty** lad (3)
- **Nick** icy winter coating (5)
- **Paloma** religious belief (5)
- **Sally** area of farmland (5)
- **Sara** type of apple (3)
- **Scott** grinds grain (5)
- **Suzi** alcoholic pear juice (5)
- **Vick** optimism (4)

MASTERCHEF

MasterChef achieved status as the preeminent amateur chef competitive television series. It became the template for a variety of subsequent cookery shows, balancing culinary tips and a tightly edited, against-the-clock competition within a genial, light entertainment atmosphere. It was the work by Franc Roddam, who had created the drama *Auf Wiedersehen, Pet* and directed the cult 1979 film *Quadrophenia*.

programmes such as *Hell's Kitchen*. It also moved from Sunday afternoon on BBC One to Tuesday night on BBC Two.

A third version of the show was launched in 2005. Resembling the talent reality shows, it ran for five nights a week across eight weeks. Its popularity also saw the launch of *Celebrity MasterChef* in 2006 and *MasterChef: The Professionals* in 2008.

For the first decade, the show comprised nine rounds, each featuring three contestants who had to create a three-course meal in two hours and within a limited budget. Winners would eventually work their way to three semi-finals and a final. The show was hosted by Lloyd Grossman and featured a guest chef and celebrity. The three would meet the contestants, discuss the menus, taste the completed meals and deliberate over each episode's winner.

The show was revamped in 2001, with new presenter chef Gary Rhodes, who had previously presented *MasterChef USA*. This time, contestants worked with the same key ingredients and had to come up with a two-course meal in 90 minutes. It took a more serious critical approach to creation of meals and, in tone, set the standard for future cookery

Lloyd Grossman with one lucky winner (top left); Gary Rhodes (above).

WINNING MENUS

Three of the winning menus from recent series of *MasterChef* have been encoded below, each in different ways. In the leftmost column the winning chefs are listed, and then their starters, mains and desserts are listed in the remaining columns. The rows within each column, however, are not in any particular order.

Each chef and their three courses have been altered in a different way, but consistently within the set. For example, one of the chefs might have had every pair of letters swapped in their name and each of their three courses. By working out the encoding methods, can you identify the chefs and their menus?

Chefs	Starters	Mains	Dessert
an evonshir	eafoo oas	Keehc xo desiarb	hubar n ustar
Ekarf Samoht	Ipmacs hsifknom	Kshmr dck	Pnn ctt
Slh Mhmd-hmd	Vnsn kbb	raise am houlde	Trat dratsuc

SPORTING CHEFS

Each of the four sportspersons pictured has won a series of *Celebrity MasterChef*. The names of these winners can be found below, but each person has been blended with the two-word name of a dish they created on the show. Despite the blending, all the letters within each word have remained in the correct order. For example, Dave + Chips might have been blended to DACVHIEPS.

Who are these winners and what did they cook?

1   2   3   4

SAMLAMTOTN   CADARWPSACCOINO

SGCROETGCH   RUETHEGRFOGRD

KTAEDMEPEUNARA   PCRAOWXN

PHLAIMBL   FIVILCLKETERY

GARDENING SHOWS

With gardening one of the country's major pastimes, it's no surprise that a gardening-themed programme germinated early at the BBC. It would become a staple of both radio and television over the course of a century, adapting to the times, but always offering top tips on what to plant and when to plant it.

Early pioneers of gardening tips in broadcasting included Vita Sackville-West and Marion Cran, whose delivery was crisp and formal, reflecting the style of the broadcaster. On 9 May 1931, C.H. Middleton broke that mould. He was chosen by the BBC from a list of potential presenters supplied by the Royal Horticultural Society to host *In Your Garden*. Welcoming audiences with a congenial 'Good afternoon. Well, it's not much of a day for gardening, is it?' Middleton's relaxed manner was new for the broadcaster and it immediately won over listeners. During the Second World War, Middleton became an essential component in encouraging the populace to grow their own food, while setting an informal, conversational template for future presenters.

The longstanding *Gardeners' Question Time* launched on the Home Service in 1947 and now has a regular slot on Radio 4. On television, Percy Thrower took the place of Middleton in 1956 with *Gardening Club* and then *Gardeners' World* in 1969. He also became a regular presence in the *Blue Peter* garden. *Gardeners' World* dominated for a few decades before the 1990s saw a variety of different approaches to the topic. Among them was *Ground Force* (1997–2005), which made Charlie Dimmock and Alan Titchmarsh household names, the latter eventually hosting *Gardeners' World*.

In Your Garden presenter C.H. Middleton discusses how to lay crazy paving in a purpose-built garden at Alexandra Palace.

FLOWER FIT

Can you plant the names of these flowers, one letter per box, into the walled garden below? There is only one way to plant all of the names so that they are each used exactly once.

4 letters
Iris
Lily
Rose

5 letters
Aster
Daisy
Phlox
Tulip

6 letters
Azalea
Crocus
Dahlia
Orchid
Violet
Zinnia

7 letters
Anemone
Begonia
Cowslip
Freesia

8 letters
Bluebell
Daffodil
Gladioli
Marigold

9 letters
Calendula
Carnation

FLOWER FIND

Hidden here is the name of a flower that uses all of the 'petal' letters once each, and the central letter twice. What is that flower?

Once you have identified the flower, see if you can also fill in the gaps in the gardening advice given. Each missing word uses letters from the flower, no more times per letter than they appear on the flower, and always includes the central letter.

1. Always grow _ _ _ _ in pots – it grows fast and might take over the garden.

2. Leek _ _ _ _ can also be a problem for garlic, onions and chives.

3. Use a trellis to _ _ _ _ _ clematis up and along a wall.

4. _ _ _ _ _ _ is the best time to plant garlic.

5. House _ _ _ _ _ _ _ are insectivores and great organic pest controllers.

CHANGING ROOMS

The 1990s saw the appearance of a new style of home-improvement show. It was less a traditional DIY-about-the-house programme than a light entertainment competitive series that offered tips on ways to make a house more stylish. Popular during its eight-year run, it was also franchised out to other countries.

The format of the show was simple. Two couples swapped houses. They then decorated one room in each other's houses. Every episode ended with the couples returning to their own homes and seeing what had been done to the decorated room. Helping the couples work on the rooms were a revolving number of top designers. Part of the pleasure in watching the programmes lay in seeing the surprise – or shock – of the couples at the moment they first see what has been done to their homes. One of the most infamous moments in the series happened when a room was designed with animal print wallpaper, leading the owners to describe it as 'a tart's boudoir'.

Starting out on BBC Two, the show first aired on 4 September 1996. For its third series in 1998, and due to its increasing popularity, the show was moved to BBC One. It remained there for another 14 series before it was cancelled in 2004. The show was hosted by Carol Smillie, who was joined by carpenter 'Handy' Andy Kane, a Cockney who brought comic relief to the proceedings, and flamboyant designer Laurence Llewelyn-Bowen, who took over from Smillie as the show's main host for series 14 and 15.

Carol Smillie presented ten series of the show, warming audiences with her cheery smile.

INTERLOCKING ROOMS

On each line below, two rooms have been 'interlocked', by taking alternate letters from the name of each room. For example, HALL and LOFT could be interlocked by taking the first and third letters of HALL, and the second and fourth letters of LOFT, to give HOLT.

Which 12 rooms have been interlocked below?

1. AOTCC

2. COLNAE

3. OAFTCY

4. NIRRERY

5. KETRHON

6. BATAROOY

PIECE IT TOGETHER

Each of the clues below describes something known by a three-letter abbreviation that in some way relates to *Changing Rooms*. Solve all the clues and enter their abbreviations horizontally into the grid, one letter per box, so that a musical instrument that can be heard in the show's catchy theme tune appears in the shaded column, reading from top to bottom. You will have to decide in which order to place the solutions into the grid.

- **Amateur home repairs**
- **Initials of one of the show's presenters, often used humorously to refer to them**
- **Material for making drainpipes and low-maintenance window frames**
- **Material made with compacted wood chips, used frequently on the show**
- **Organization that first transmitted the show**
- **Type of glue used frequently in craft projects**

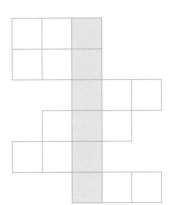

News, Weather and Current Affairs

News and weather have become such an essential part of broadcasting schedules, it is difficult to conceive that in the early days their roles were limited. Newspapers feared the impact broadcast news would have on their sales, so no reports were permitted until after 7pm every day. Things changed with the 1926 General Strike and the BBC briefly became the sole channel for the nation's news. From there, it gradually increased its role in reporting on key events, amassing a small army of journalists, despatched around the world, giving us up-to-the-minute reports of events as they unfolded. Accompanying them are analyses and discussions on politics and current affairs, from coverage of Parliament and general elections to public-facing interviews grappling with the issues of the day. Initially, weather reports were considered to be of interest only to those directly affected by it, through programmes like the shipping news. But nowadays, with advances in technology, we are informed regularly of the slightest fluctuations in weather conditions from region to region, as well as internationally.

NEWS HISTORY

The BBC began with the news. Its first radio broadcast was a news bulletin. Ever since, news has played a vital role across the landscape of the corporation, from radio and television to online platforms and podcasts.

The first news report was aired on 14 November 1922. At the time, to avoid competition with newspapers, the government agreed that no news could be broadcast before 7pm each day. It wasn't until the outbreak of the Second World War that news could be broadcast before 6pm. On 9 October 1945, the first edition of *Today in Parliament* was broadcast. The following year, radio bulletins were broadcast via television, albeit with audiences only seeing a still image of Big Ben on their screens.

On television, independently produced newsreels had been broadcast since 1936, but the corporation had to wait until 1948 to launch its own *Television Newsreel* programme.

This was followed in 1950 by the *Children's Newsreel*. Regular televised bulletins by the BBC followed in 1954. As the 1960s progressed, national news coverage was accompanied by regional news reports and programmes, while, in 1968, *Newsroom* was the first current affairs programme to be broadcast in colour.

The first edition of the *BBC Nine O'Clock News* was aired in 1970. Live coverage of the House of Commons began in 1989, which became more extensive with the launch of BBC Parliament in 1998. BBC News Online and BBC News 24 were launched in 1997, and began their transformation of news consumption in the UK and the wider world. They gained initial traction through the general election results and the response to Princess Diana's death, but speedily became the digital driver of the BBC's future.

John Craven (sitting centre) presented the first BBC news programme specially made for children, *John Craven's Newsround*.

NEWS NEWS NEWS

Given below are the incomplete names of BBC news programmes past and present, all of which include the word 'News' in their name. To the right, the missing parts of each show's title have had their letters jumbled. Unscramble each jumbled word and then match it to the correct show, based on the given descriptions.

1. _____ *News*: BBC Three entertainment news roundup from 2000–04

2. *News* _____ _____ : Lunchtime news on BBC One from 1981–86

3. *News*_____ : News programme for BBC Radio 1 and BBC Radio 1Xtra

4. *News*_____ : Podcast covering political events, from 2020 onwards

5. *News*_____ : Weekday current affairs, started 1980, currently broadcast on BBC Two

6. *News*_____ : BBC Two's main news show, the first shown in colour, from 1964–72

7. *News*_____ : News programme for children, broadcast since 1972

8. *News*_____ : Programme responding to viewer comments about BBC News coverage

9. _____ *News*: News programme created entirely from material sent in by viewers

ACTS

BETA

FERAT ONNO

MOOR

NOURD

QUIDIL

ROUY

THAWC

THING

WHEN THE NEWS WAS NEW

Arthur Burrows began the first-ever news broadcast with the words '2LO, Marconi House, London calling' – giving the address he was broadcasting from. But what happened next?

Use the clues below to determine an order of appearance for five of the items read out during the first ever broadcast.

- The coverage of the **train robbery** was not the first item on the broadcast
- The **weather forecast** was read out immediately after the **billiards scores**
- The report of the **'rowdy' meeting involving Winston Churchill** was broadcast before the **reported sale of a rare Shakespearean folio**
- The **train robbery** coverage was read out before the **weather forecast**
- The **reported sale of a rare Shakespearean folio** was the third item in the bulletin

THE TODAY PROGRAMME

For four decades, Radio 4's start-of-the-day news programme has not just been one of the station's most listened-to programmes, it has been an essential daily overview of British and international news, a barometer of the British political climate and, on many an occasion, has attracted controversy and the ire of politicians who have come unstuck during one of the show's interview segments.

The show was launched on the BBC Home Service on 28 October 1957. Founded by Janet Quigley and Isa Benzie – the latter giving the show its name and acting as its first editor – *Today*'s original remit was to present listeners with a topical alternative to light music programming. It was merged into the BBC's Current Affairs department in 1963 and, with it, the tone of the show became more news-oriented. By the late 1960s it had extended to two hours long, eventually becoming three hours on weekdays and two on a Saturday.

In 1958, Jack de Manio became *Today*'s principal presenter, remaining on the show until 1971. John Timpson and Brian Redhead's stint throughout the 1970s helped consolidate *Today*'s profile. And Gillian Reynolds became the first female presenter in 1975. But it was with news that Prime Minister Margaret Thatcher tuned in during the 1980s that *Today* became essential listening and a powerhouse of political, social and cultural reporting, which it has continued to maintain. The show has become known for its combative style, especially with lead presenter John Humphrys, who took on the great and good of the political world, holding them to account on behalf of the listener.

John Humphrys (left) was a *Today* presenter for 32 years; Lenny Henry (right), here with former footballer Chris Hughton, was guest editor in 2014.

SUE-DOKU

Place one of A, C, E, G, M, O, R, S and T into each empty square, so that no letter repeats in any row, column or bold-lined 3×3 box. Once the puzzle is solved, the surname of a well-known *Today* presenter will be revealed in the shaded squares, reading down from the top-left corner.

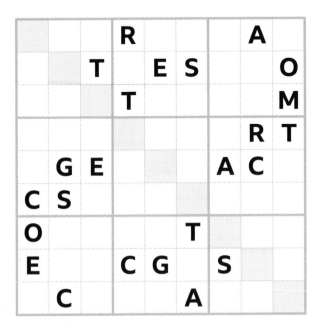

THE SCHEDULE FOR TODAY

Described below is a schedule for a hypothetical *Today* broadcast. Can you sort the six feature items into their chronological broadcast order, based on the information given?

- The **political discussion** was not the last item
- The **business news** was discussed before **Thought for the Day**
- The newspaper headlines were discussed before the **business news**
- The **interview with a supermarket CEO** was aired after the **weather forecast**
- The **business news** was covered immediately after the **weather forecast**
- The **CEO interview** was immediately followed by the **political discussion**

POLITICAL INTERVIEWS

The way television and radio covered politics since the latter half of the 20th century has changed significantly. What might once have been a cosy and polite conversation has developed over the years into a form of sparring, with the occasional drawing of blood – metaphorically, at least – that can often resemble a gladiatorial battle of words.

The years that followed the Second World War saw the continuation of a deferential approach to political figures in the media. But a new generation of journalists gradually changed the tone. If an interviewer like Ludovic Kennedy chose a style of friendly banter to get his subjects to talk, a more probing approach was adopted by Robin Day, who set the template for the confrontational interview style. As media coverage of everyday life grew more expansive and politicians attempted to use it as a platform to air their views, so journalists intensified their interrogation of those in positions of power.

From Richard, David and Jonathan Dimbleby to Jenni Murray, John Humphrys and Jeremy Paxman, changing interviewing techniques gave journalists more scope to pressure politicians for answers. Some proved more amenable than others. Whereas Labour Prime Minister Harold Wilson enjoyed sparring, Margaret Thatcher determinedly remained on point, only ever answering with what she planned to say.

Of the most famous interviews, two stand out. Jeremy Paxman's 1997 *Newsnight* interview with the then Home Secretary saw him ask variations of the same question 12 times. Even more impressive was English schoolteacher Diana Gold's interrogation of Margaret Thatcher about the sinking of the Argentinian Navy's *General Belgrano* cruiser during the Falklands War. This happened on *Newsnight*, during the 1983 General Election campaign, and remains one of the few times the former prime minister looked flummoxed on air.

Former leader of the Conservative Party Michael Howard prepares for an interview with Jeremy Paxman.

ORDER OF THE DAYS

Sort these major events into chronological order, starting with the oldest first. Once arranged correctly, the numbers at the end of each line can be read in order to reveal the date of the first *Newsnight* broadcast, in the form DD/MM/YYYY.

- **David Cameron forms a coalition government:** 9
- **Falklands War begins:** 0
- **Margaret Thatcher resigns:** 1
- **National Health Service is established:** 3
- **Scottish independence referendum returns a 'no' vote:** 8
- **Tony Blair's 'New Labour' wins a landslide general election:** 1
- **UK joins the European Economic Community:** 0
- **UK votes to leave the EU:** 0

DODGE THE QUESTION

How well would you do at avoiding giving a too-revealing answer to a question during a political interview? Find out by discovering the location of – and therefore avoiding – all of the tricky questions hiding in the grid below.

Numbers reveal the exact number of questions hiding in adjacent squares, including diagonally. Mark each hidden question with a '?' – so you know to avoid it. No more than one '?' is hidden per square, and none of the squares with numbers contain a '?'.

		3		3			2
2	3				3	3	
2		4			2		2
	3		2		2		
2		4	4			2	
				4			2
3			6		3		
2		4				2	

SATIRE

Although satire had been a staple of British social and political life for centuries, in television it fully emerged with changing attitudes during the 1960s. And once the floodgates opened, the surge of satirical comedies has rarely let up.

The first wave of satirists to benefit from the wide appeal of television emerged from the success of the stage show *Beyond the Fringe* in 1960. Written by, and starring, Peter Cook, Dudley Moore, Alan Bennett and Jonathan Miller, it offered audiences a review that pushed further in its dissection of contemporary British life. Around the same time, Cook launched his Soho nightclub The Establishment and *Private Eye* was founded. Producer Ned Sherrin, picking up on the disaffection exhibited by a significant proportion of British society following the Suez Crisis debacle, commissioned the magazine show *That Was the Week That Was* (1962–63), which skewered political and social life. It lasted only a year, but its impact could be seen in subsequent series, from *The Frost Report* (1966–67) to *Have I Got News for You* (1990) and *Mock the Week* (2005).

A scene from *Yes, Minister*.

The Thick of It, starring Peter Capaldi.

A more surreal edge was introduced at the end of the 1960s by the hugely influential *Monty Python's Flying Circus* (1969–74). It was followed by *Not the Nine O'Clock News* (1979–82) and *A Kick Up the Eighties* (1981–84), whose acerbic take on politics and culture was later reflected in *The Day Today* (1994) and Charlie Brooker's *Wipe* series, which began in 2006. However, arguably the most successful skewering of the British political class was carried out by the series *Yes, Minister* and *Yes, Prime Minister* (1980–88) and *The Thick of It* (2005–12).

The team from *Not the Nine O'Clock News*, from left to right: Mel Smith, Pamela Stephenson, Rowan Atkinson and Griff Rhys Jones.

HAVE I GOT PRESENTERS FOR YOU

Have I Got News For You has featured guest presenting, along with the number of letters in their name as it is normally credited. Can you identify all nine guest presenters, then answer the questions below?
presenters since 2002, although some of them have appeared many times. Nine of these guest presenters are clued below by the name of another BBC show that they are well-known for

1. *Desert Island Discs* (6, 5)
2. *Match of the Day* (4, 7)
3. *Mock the Week* (4, 1, 6)
4. *Only Connect* (8, 5, 8)
5. *Pointless* (9, 9)
6. *Question Time* (5, 8)
7. *The Great British Bake Off: An Extra Slice* (2, 5)
8. *The Weakest Link* (4, 8)
9. *Top Gear* (6, 8)

A. Which of these presenters has hosted the most *HIGNFY* episodes, as of the start of 2022?
B. Can you identify which one of these presenters was the first guest to make their debut appearance as a guest host, rather than as a guest panellist?
C. Which guest presenter (not clued above) went on to become prime minister?

LORD PRIVY SEAL

In a, now famous, *The Frost Report* sketch, the presenter poked fun at the television trope of accompanying spoken reports with an unnecessarily large number of illustrative images. In this particular sketch, the mention of the parliamentary role of 'Lord Privy Seal' is
accompanied by three images; one of a Lord, one of an outdoor privy, and finally a seal in a circus. Using the above joke as an example, can you guess which parliamentary roles are being clued on each line below? Each image clues one word.

1

2

3

4

ELECTION NIGHT

Elections are an essential element in the fabric of any democracy. Since the 1950s, television has played a key role in chronicling political party campaigns and election night itself, reporting on the results as they are announced. The BBC has been a pioneer not only in employing its resources to cover the results across the United Kingdom, but also in how election night is structured and presented.

Before television became involved, British audiences heard the results of the election via a radio announcer. But in 1950, television producer Grace Wyndham Goldie and journalist Chester Wilmot conceived the first election night broadcast, featuring coverage of the election results and discussion of their

implications. Fully aware of the power of the medium, Goldie wanted to offer audiences 'the unmistakable feeling of direct experience'. On 23 February 1950, after polling stations had closed and the counting of votes began, this is what audiences witnessed for the first time. The impact increased with the 1955 election, if only because more households owned a television.

Richard Dimbleby, one of the most influential figures in broadcast journalism, presented three election night programmes, setting a high standard that was continued by his son David. In 1959, the 'swingometer' offered audiences the first visual guide to how the election was progressing. Computers were introduced in 1966, with colour following in 1970. And in 1983, Peter Snow made his first appearance, a man closely associated with the increasingly digitized display screens, which replaced the more rudimentary swingometer. And although technology has made election night slicker, that format devised by Goldie and perfected by Richard Dimbleby remains in place.

David Dimbleby (left) has hosted every general election night since 1979; the *Newsround* team with Peter Snow in 1997 (above).

ORDER, ORDER

Fill in the grid with the surnames of all of the UK prime ministers (as of the start of 2022) that have been in power since the BBC's second election night broadcast in 1951. Write each answer horizontally, with one letter per box. The numbers to the left of each row indicate the order of their election to PM, where '1' is the earliest. But:

• Do not include the only prime minister during this period who was in office for less than one year.

• One prime minister served two non-consecutive terms, so they are included twice.

2
7
13
9
12
4
14
11
10
5
8
1
3
6

SWINGOMETER SWINGS

Eight political words or phrases have been subject to a verbal swingometer – which in this case means that they have had each of their letters shifted a number of places forwards (to the right) or backwards (to the left) through the alphabet. The word 'POLL' shifted two places forward, for example, would become RQNN. Anything shifting before A or after Z has 'wrapped around' to the other end of the alphabet.

Can you decode all of the election jargon below? Those marked 'Labour' have swung to the left, and those marked 'Conservative' have swung to the right. None of the swings are by more than five letters.

1. **HALW SROO** (Conservative)

2. **LKNPEHHK IKIAJP** (Labour)

3. **XJFY** (Conservative)

4. **KYHMPGRW** (Labour)

5. **IVOH QBSMJBNFOU** (Conservative)

6. **DKDBSHNM** (Labour)

7. **ZXJMXFDK** (Labour)

8. **OCPKHGUVQ** (Conservative)

ROYAL EVENTS

Just as the royal family has played a perennial role in British life, their link with the BBC and its coverage of royal events dates back almost to the broadcaster's inception. And over the course of a century, royal events have broken new ground and records.

The first official broadcast by a member of the royal family took place on 23 April 1924, when King George V opened the Empire Exhibition at Wembley Stadium. He was also the first monarch to deliver a Christmas message, via the Empire (now World) Service, in 1932. Twenty-five years later, his granddaughter, Queen Elizabeth II, who was just 14 when she made her first radio broadcast in 1940, delivered the first televised Christmas message. Other annual events featuring the Queen have included the

Armistice Day Remembrance ceremony, the 29 January Beating Retreat ceremony, and Trooping the Colour, which marks the official birthday of the British sovereign.

An outside broadcasting van was first used for coverage of the procession that followed the coronation of King George VI and Queen Elizabeth in 1937. It was followed a decade later by the wedding of Princess Elizabeth and Philip Mountbatten, Duke of Edinburgh, which attracted an audience of 400,000. This was dwarfed by the coronation of Queen Elizabeth II in Westminster Abbey on 2 June 1953, which saw an estimated British audience of 20 million tune in. By the time of Prince Charles and Princess Diana's wedding on 29 July 1981, an estimated worldwide audience of 750 million were watching.

An incredible 28.4 million Britons watched the wedding of Prince Charles to Lady Diana Spencer – 600,000 on the streets of London and the rest on the BBC.

THE CARRIAGE RIDE

Some of the most iconic images of the British monarchy show members of the royal family travelling to and from royal events in an open-top carriage. Can you plan a circular route for just such an event?

Draw a single loop that visits every white square in the grid to the right exactly once each, including the squares marked with a carriage and a cathedral. The loop can't enter any of the black squares.

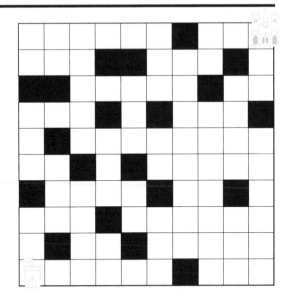

WEDDING BELLS

Four royal weddings which have been covered by the BBC are shown below – although the faces of each couple have been obscured. Can you use your judgement to work out which pair have just tied the knot in each photo?

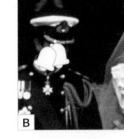

BBC WEATHER

Come rain or shine, the BBC has informed the nation of weather conditions since 1922. Forecasts were supplied by the British government's Met Office until 2018, when responsibility shifted to MeteoGroup.

Across the course of a century, audiences have witnessed seismic changes in the accuracy of weather reports and how technology has shifted in the way they are reported, from symbols stuck – and occasionally slipping off – a map of the United Kingdom to the latest in digital imagery.

The first broadcast was the shipping news, which took place on 14 November 1922, while the first daily weather forecast took place on 26 March 1923. The first televised weather map screened as early as 1936, but it wasn't until 1949 that they became a regular fixture. At this point, the forecaster was only heard through a voiceover. On-screen presenters appeared in 1954, beginning with George Cowling. His approach was more formal, but over the course of subsequent decades, forecasters' personalities would shine through, making presenters such as Michael Fish, Barbara Edwards – the first female forecaster, who began on BBC Radio in 1970 – and Ian McCaskill household names.

Initially, weather forecasters drew their own maps. The introduction of faxes and rudimentary computers in the early 1960s helped with accuracy, along with satellite photography from 1964. For years, forecasters placed magnetized icons denoting a certain weather condition on a board, before a major change in 2005 saw computer-generated imagery allowing for more detailed analysis of climactic changes.

Carol Kirkwood is one of the BBC's most experienced and popular weather presenters, best known for her work on BBC Breakfast.

WHATEVER THE WEATHER

Can you use the map below to identify the varying weather forecasts for different areas of Great Britain? Start at the yellow square with the 'W', and move horizontally or vertically from square to square, tracing out a continuous path that visits each letter of the grid exactly once, spelling out various types of weather as you go. That path should finish in London, marked with the green square.

Once the weather has all been revealed, use your geographical knowledge to answer the questions beneath.

1. **Which of these three counties seems likely to receive the most snow?**
   a. Essex
   b. North Yorkshire
   c. Gloucestershire

2. **What two weather phenomena can be expected along the Scottish border?**

3. **Which Scottish city is more likely to have good visibility: Aberdeen or Fort William?**

4. **What type of weather should primarily be expected in Lincolnshire?**

SHIPPING FORECAST

This broadcast of weather reports, forecasts and details of sea conditions around the coast of the British Isles employs a language that occasionally sounds arcane and could be mistaken for code. Although only required by a limited number of people, the forecasts have proven incredibly popular, attracting audiences in their hundreds of thousands.

Produced by the Met Office for Radio 4 on behalf of the Maritime and Coastguard Agency, broadcasts are made four times a day, at 00:48, 05:20, 12:01 and 17:54, on longwave, with the first two broadcasts also available on FM and the last broadcast on FM each weekend. The waters around the British Isles are divided into 31 sea areas, whose names run from the obvious (Humber, Thames, Plymouth, Irish Sea, Hebrides) to the less familiar (Viking, Forties, Dogger, German Bight, FitzRoy, Fastnet, Malin, Bailey). They were created in 1949, with additions and changes to names introduced by meteorologists in 1955. The names reference sandbanks, estuaries and islands.

Each broadcast details, in order, any gale warnings, a general overview of the weather and specific forecasts for each of the areas. Each forecast is limited to a set number of words, which is strictly adhered to. (The 00:48 broadcast is extended to 380 words, to include Trafalgar, the coastal area to the west of Spain.) The broadcast begins with conditions off the northeast coast of Scotland then journeys clockwise around the British Isles until it reaches its final destination, Southeast Iceland. And the unhurried and unfazed style of presentation, maintaining a consistent tone, has found it sampled in the music of Blur, Radiohead and The Prodigy.

For skippers of vessels in waters around the coast of Britian, the *Shipping Forecast* is a regular and reliable source of local weather conditions.

SEA AREAS

Below is a map of the sea areas featured on the *Shipping Forecast*, although the name labels have been removed from each area and are instead listed either side of the map. Can you use your general knowledge to match each name to its correct location?

Bailey

Biscay

Cromarty

Dogger

Dover

Faeroes

Fair Isle

Fastnet

Fisher

FitzRoy

Forth

Forties

German Bight

Hebrides

Humber

Irish Sea

Lundy

Malin

North Utsire

Plymouth

Portland

Rockall

Shannon

Sole

South Utsire

Southeast Iceland

Thames

Trafalgar

Tyne

Viking

Wight

SHIPPING FORECAST TRIVIA

1. What is the name of the instrumental piece played at the end of the 0048 broadcast?
2. Which sea area was once known as Finisterre?
3. What is the maximum word limit for any of the forecasts?
4. Stornoway, Jersey and Bridlington might all feature in the *Shipping Forecast*. What are they, in that context?

REGIONAL AND NATIONAL NEWS

Although the BBC began broadcasting from London in 1922, it soon branched out to ensure some kind of regional broadcast structure was in place. However, in spite of the societal changes that occurred in the United Kingdom over the subsequent 50 years, by the late 1960s that structure remained. Then a new official report created the impetus for change in both the BBC's national and regional programming.

The BBC's original structure divided England into four regions – BBC North, BBC Midlands and East Anglia, BBC South and West, and London, which wasn't so much a region as it was the main service for the other areas. In addition to this, Scotland, Wales and Northern Ireland also had their own transmission hubs.

The publication of the 'Broadcasting in the Seventies' report in 1969 proposed a new and exciting future for BBC programmes. The BBC national radio networks were further refined to reflect new listening habits, and the BBC affirmed its strong commitment to the BBC Local Radio network.

In England, the BBC adopted smaller regional areas, each with its own news programme. At the same time, from the late 1960s onwards, there was an evolution of BBC Local Radio – beginning with Leicester in 1967 and developing into an eventual network of 40 stations in England and the Channel Islands.

The structure adopted in the 1970s has remained relatively the same, save for the occasional region dividing into smaller areas as a result of digital technology reducing the cost of creating new services.

BBC Scotland operates BBC One Scotland, its own BBC Scotland channel and the dedicated Gaelic-language channel BBC Alba.

LOST IN THE AIRWAVES

Each of the local English TV news programmes listed below is headquartered in a location somewhere within its catchment area. Can you match each programme with the name of the city or town on the left that serves as its headquarters? Every second letter has been removed in the names of the locations in order to disguise them.

Headquarters location:

1. B_I_T_L
2. _A_C_E_T_R
3. B_R_I_G_A_
4. _E_D_
5. C_M_R_D_E
6. N_T_I_G_A_
7. _L_M_U_H
8. L_N_O_
9. _T _E_I_R
10. R_Y_L _U_B_I_G_ W_L_S
11. S_U_H_M_T_N

News programme:

BBC Channel Islands

BBC East Midlands Today

BBC London News

BBC Look East

BBC Look North

BBC Midlands Today

BBC North West Tonight

BBC Points West

BBC South East Today

BBC South Today

BBC Spotlight

HOME SWEET HOME

The headquarters of BBC Scotland moved to a new building in 2007, opened by then Prime Minister Gordon Brown. Can you trace out the name of the new building in the grid below, by moving from square to square in any direction, including diagonally, one letter at a time? The name consists of three words, and each square is used once.

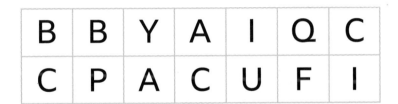

B	B	Y	A	I	Q	C
C	P	A	C	U	F	I

In addition, can you spot seven three-letter words that can be spelled out in the grid?

WORLD SERVICE

From humble beginnings, with the BBC's own Director-General Lord Reith stating, 'Don't expect too much in the early days . . . the programmes will neither be very interesting nor very good', the World Service is now the world's largest international broadcasting operation, with a reach as diverse as the programmes it presents.

Broadcasting for 24 hours a day via both analogue and digital shortwave platforms, as well as streaming via the Internet, podcasts and a variety of satellite, DAB, FM and MW relays, the World Service reaches more than 489 million people worldwide, across television, radio and online.

It has eight main feeds that encompass the United Kingdom, East and South Africa, West and Central Africa, Europe and the Middle East, the Americas and Caribbean, East Asia, South Asia and Australasia. It began airing on 19 December 1932 as the BBC Empire Service. With its expansion during the Second World War, in which it played a pivotal role (from relaying messages to overseas agents, to George Orwell's broadcasts across the Eastern Service), it became known as the BBC Overseas Service. In 1965, it was given its current name.

King George V summed up the service's remit in his first address across its airwaves when he described it as being for 'men and women, so cut off by the snow, the desert, or the sea, that only voices out of the air can reach them'. Across its history, the service has been broadcast in 80 different languages or dialects. Today, it broadcasts in 40 languages, including Amharic, the official language of Ethiopia, and Nigerian Igbo, introduced as part of the last expansion in 2016.

Sourour Effendi, the famous announcer of the BBC Arabic Service, the BBC's first foreign language service, launched in 1938.

LIST IN TRANSLATION

Listed below are eight of the various languages that BBC World Service has broadcast in, but these languages are spelled as a native of those countries would write them. Can you identify which languages they are, and match each language with the outline of the European country it is most widely spoken in? Note that the country outlines are not to scale.

- **Čeština**
- **Français**
- **Hrvatski**
- **Italiano**
- **Magyar**
- **Nederlands**
- **Polski**
- **Suomi**

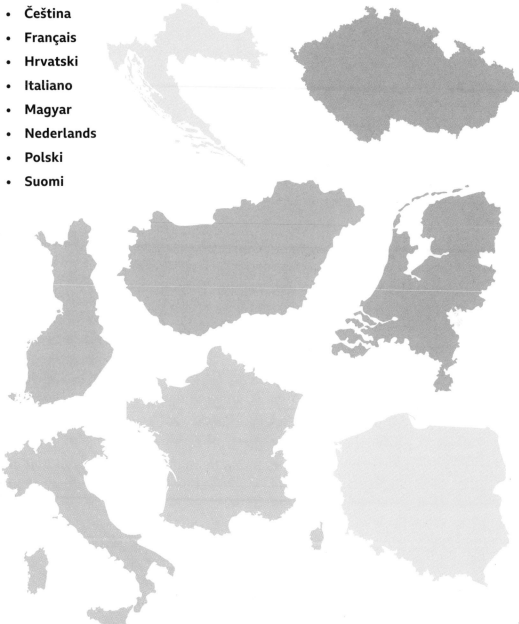

Technology

The BBC could not function without technology. But with the passage of time, the broadcaster shifted from being a body that embraced new innovations to being the innovator that helped usher them in. As it expanded in scale, the BBC sought new ways of utilizing transmitters to reach every home around the British Isles. As a result, the number of local news stations has multiplied over the decades, while experiments in visual technology have seen television shift from the margins to become the primary receptor for news, information, media-based education and entertainment. As the world switched from analogue to digital, the broadcaster followed suit, both from an operational perspective and user interactivity. The nature of broadcasting changed; where the BBC once decided what audiences could hear or watch at a given time, control was placed in the hands of each individual, giving them the option to enjoy their favourite programme at a time to suit them.

DIGITAL WORLD

The BBC had long engaged with a level of technological interactivity with audiences, from the launch of Ceefax in 1974 through to computing in the 1980s. The development of the Internet and rapid digitalization of media around the world saw the broadcaster further embrace a new age in broadcasting just as the world was entering a new millennium.

The BBC's first entry into the online world was in 1994, when it launched the BBC Networking Club, an early social networking site. It was relaunched as BBC Online in 1997. (It was also briefly known as BBCi and bbc.co.uk.) In September 1995, the BBC began regular Digital Audio Broadcasting, in addition to its usual frequencies, from its Crystal Palace transmitting station in south London. In 1997, it sold its transmitters and transmission services in order to raise money for its full embrace of the

PAGE | SPORT | WEATHER | WORLD SERVICE | MY BBC

NEWS

Tuesday, 11 September, 2001, 20:40 GMT 21:40 UK

US rocked by terror attacks

Thousands are feared dead after a series of devastating attacks targeting the USA's financial and military centres in New York and Washington.

Also:
- Cockpit drama of doomed planes
- World shock at attacks
- Security alerts spread from US
- Who might have done it?
- Timeline: America rocked by explosions
- **Talking Point:** Send us your eyewitness accounts
- **In Depth:** America attacked

Eyewitnesses tell of horror

People on the scene of America's disasters describe extraordinary scenes of panic and terror.

Also:
- Eyewitness: The twin towers fall
- Britons tell of New York horror
- Hospitals receive flood of victims

digital age. Later in the year, BBC News Online and BBC Online were launched. BBC Choice, launched in September 1998, became the first service available only via digital TV services. It was followed by BBC Knowledge and BBC Text.

BBC Online has remained hugely popular, although its scope has been reduced over the 2000s in order to prevent it enjoying a monopoly over commercial rivals. This has seen various radio stations and online activity fluctuate over the past two decades, but it remains one of the United Kingdom's main sources of news, music and entertainment.

BBC News Online (above); Bob Eggington and Mike Smartt of BBC News Online collect their BAFTA for Best News Website in 1999 (left).

LOST IN THE WEB

Find the names of the main sections of the BBC Online website in the grid below by moving from letter to letter, spelling out each section as you go. Diagonal moves are not allowed, and each square should be visited exactly once. The path starts by tracing out 'NEWS', and ends at the yellow square. There are 10 further sections to find.

P	L	A	Y	S	O	L	O
I	R	E	E	R	U	E	C
A	T	H	S	D	N	Z	A
E	B	B	C	E	S	I	L
W	C	C	B	T	I	A	T
T	P	S	E	D	B	S	T
R	O	S	E	O	O	F	E
N	E	W	B	I	E	S	R

SECTION SELECTION

Can you work out which section each of the listed page titles featured under on the BBC Online site? Each is from a different section revealed in the puzzle above, but none of them are from 'News'.

1. **'Check out this incredible rainbow fish!'**

2. **'F1 releases new overtaking guidelines'**

3. **'Pack Mr Bumble's spotty bag'**

4. **'Should extinct species be brought back to life?'**

5. **'Slow cooker hacks to save you money and effort'**

6. **'Strange UFO clouds spotted over Cumbria'**

COMPUTING

The emergence of the home computer at the end of the 1970s was a revolution in technology. The BBC not only sought to lead the way in the development of home-use computer technology, but was also perfectly placed to promote its benefits within the national education system. For a while, the BBC microcomputer was as close as most homes got to state-of-the-art computing.

At the beginning of the 1980s, the broadcaster created the BBC Computer Literacy Project. Its aim was to introduce audiences to a new age, highlighting the profound impact computers would likely – and did – have on every aspect of our lives, from the schoolroom to the home and the workplace. The idea was to develop a microcomputer that would be affordable for the average family and that would encourage computer literacy. Several technology companies were approached by the BBC to design the computer, with the contract being awarded to Acorn Computers, whose prototype, known as Proton, far exceeded expectations and its competitors. Leading the design group were computer scientists Sophie Wilson and Steve Furber.

Further research and development resulted in the release of the BBC Microcomputer on 1 December 1981. The following year, it was accompanied by *The Computer Programme*, hosted by Chris Searle, which explored the possibilities of the computer and answered viewers' queries. The computers were hugely popular, with around 80 per cent of British schools owning one.

Six BBC Micro models were produced, with remaining versions of the computer coming under the aegis of Acorn's Archimedes series. They were invaluable in helping to introduce families and schools to what would become an increasingly virtual world.

Ian McNaught-Davis, co-presenter of *The Computer Programme*, known as 'Mac' for short.

BASIC WORD PUZZLE

BBC Micros came with the programming language BBC BASIC built in, which introduced generations of British schoolchildren to coding. Can you fit all of the listed BBC BASIC keywords into the grid, crossword-style with one letter per box? Ignore any spaces when entering the keywords.

2-letter words
IF
LN
OR
PI

3-letter words
ASC
CLG
CLS
DEF
DEG
DIM
DIV
ERR
EXP
INT
LEN
MOD
NEW
NOT
POS
RUN
SGN
SIN
SPC
VAL

4-letter words
DATA
ELSE
EVAL
GCOL
NEXT
STOP

5-letter words
CHAIN
CLOSE
LOCAL

6-letter words
ON GOTO
OPENIN

8-letter words
ENVELOPE

INTERACTIVE

Interactivity, the engagement of the BBC with its viewers, was a key element for the broadcaster long before the digital age. But the ability of audiences to choose from the BBC's services has only increased with the rising sophistication of technology, although these days, one of its most popular innovations might seem more than a little rudimentary.

Before the BBC Red Button and iPlayer, offering viewers wider choice regarding information and programming, there was Ceefax. Its functioning was simple. A viewer pressed the Ceefax button on their remote and then typed in a three-digit number that would take them to a specific page. The technology was created, in part, as a way of providing hearing-impaired viewers with subtitles. An adaptation of a previous text transmission analogue printing service, it soon

allowed viewers to scroll through news and a wide variety of information. Launched in 1974, it remained in operation until 23 October 2012. The Red Button Service launched as BBC Text on 23 September 1999 (it was rebranded as BBC Red Button in 2008). It performed a similar service to Ceefax, but with more interactivity and a richer, more varied interface. It also allowed viewers to continue watching a programme while part of the screen was taken up with additional information.

BBC iPlayer, a video-on-demand service, went live on Christmas Day 2007, with upgrades following over the next decade. Just as Ceefax increased viewers' interactivity at the dawn of the home computer age, so iPlayer became an essential part of British viewers' lives just as streaming was changing the way we consume home entertainment.

Ceefax (above and top right): a pun on 'seeing facts', this was the world's first teletext information service.

TRUE OR FALSE?

Can you work out whether each of the following statements about BBC iPlayer is true or false? Collect the letter next to your chosen answer on each line, and if they are all correct then they will spell out (from top to bottom) the name of the most-watched TV programme on iPlayer in 2009.

1. A 2009 press release published on 1 April claimed that iPlayer users would be able to watch BBC shows on a specially engineered toaster with an LED screen – **TRUE 'T', FALSE 'N'**

2. The volume control on the BBC iPlayer webpage goes up to 12 – **TRUE 'I', FALSE 'O'**

3. Coverage of the Ashes was the most popular radio content accessed in 2009 – **TRUE 'P', FALSE 'M'**

4. International versions of BBC iPlayer were launched in Europe with some programmes made by other channels such as ITV and Channel 4 – **TRUE 'G', FALSE 'B'**

5. BBC Store – an online service for viewers to purchase downloadable content – was initially given the codename 'Project Lisbon' – **TRUE 'L', FALSE 'E'**

6. As of 2016, viewers have not needed a TV licence to watch BBC iPlayer content – **TRUE 'O', FALSE 'A'**

7. 'Making the unmissable, unmissable' was one of the service's taglines in its early days – **TRUE 'R', FALSE 'S'**

PICK A NUMBER

See if you can work out which three-digit number you would have had to type in to visit each of the following Ceefax pages, based on the given clues. For all of the puzzles, the numbers are imagined as though displayed on a digital clock, composed of straight horizontal and vertical lines. None of the numbers are less than 100.

1. **News headlines:** A palindromic number whose digits added up to 2, and which would appear the same if read upside down or in a mirror.
2. **Subtitles:** Three numbers that all appear the same when read upside down, in a mirror, and even when upside down in a mirror!
3. **National Lottery Results:** Three identical numbers that appear the same if read upside down. If read in a mirror placed at the right-hand side of the screen, however, it would appear as a number 333 lower than itself.
4. **Main index:** A number that was lower than the number for the news headlines page.
5. **Sport index (from the late 80s onwards):** If this number was viewed in a mirror, placed horizontally along the centre of the number, it would look the same. It was also a whole multiple of both 6 and 25.

Answers

Page 13: BBC Radio
Three Counties
Buckinghamshire, Bedfordshire, Hertfordshire

Local Legends
From top left to bottom right:
Sara Cox: BBC Radio Manchester
Lauren Laverne: BBC Radio Newcastle
Annie Nightingale: BBC Radio London
Edith Bowman: BBC Radio Scotland
Tommy Vance: BBC Radio Oxford
Chris Moyles: BBC Radio Leeds

Page 15: BBC TV
Media Match

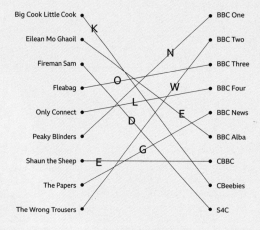

The highlighted letters spell KNOWLEDGE. BBC Knowledge is a former BBC channel that was later replaced by BBC Four.

Ident Identity
Top left: BBC Two
Top right: BBC Four
Bottom left: BBC One
Bottom right: BBC News

Page 19: The Talk Show
The Guest List

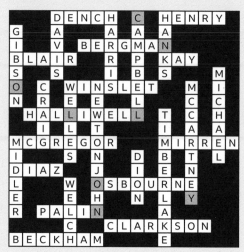

The shaded letters can be rearranged to spell out the surname of Billy CONNOLLY, the show's most featured guest.

The Name of the Game
The show titles are shown in capitals:
CILLA Black (69 episodes)
Jeremy CLARKSON (27 episodes)
DAVINA McCall (8 episodes)
ESTHER Rantzen (Over 600 episodes)
Terry WOGAN (1,131 episodes)
RUBY Wax (48 episodes)

Page 21: The *Radio Times*
Schedule Switch
From top to bottom, the years of first publication are 1937, 1969, 2005, 1994, 1923, 1946 and 1928. Arranging these in chronological order, and then writing the numbers next to them in that same order, gives the date 8/10/1960. The listings for this day were in two magazines since the publication changed from being listed Sunday to Saturday to a new format of Saturday to Friday.

The Test of Times
1. Television listings, as TV was stopped during the Second World War and did not restart until 7 June 1946.
2. *Doctor Who*

3. The 'Toddlers' Truce' – the gap began after children's programming and before the evening schedule
4. 1957
5. BBC Two
6. 2003

Page 23: Variety Shows
Mystery Clues
The solutions are all the surnames of *Royal Variety* hosts, known as MCs. The words and the hosts they represent are as follows:
1. Bob HOPE (1977)
2. Cilla BLACK (1993)
3. David FROST (1991)
4. Jack WHITEHALL (2015)
5. John BISHOP (2013)
6. Miranda HART (2017)

The hint from the puzzle title is that its initials are also 'MC'.

Bits and Pieces
Acrobatics; Comedy; Dance; Juggling; Magic; Music; Ventriloquism

The Stars
All of the band names follow the format, 'The _____s'. From left to right, the bands are:
The Beatles; The Supremes; The Shadows; The Killers

Page 25: Popular Shows
A Host of Talent
QI, hosted by Sandi Toksvig (3)
Pointless, hosted by Alexander Armstrong (4)
Would I Lie to You?, hosted by Rob Brydon (2)
The Weakest Link, hosted by Romesh Ranganathan (1)
All four of the hosts have been a guest host on *Have I Got News for You*.

Blankety Blank
Lenny Henry
Ian McKellan
Des Lynham
Esme Young
Spike Milligan
Anneka Rice
Johnny Vegas
Angela Rippon
Gloria Gaynor
Sophie Ellis-Bextor

The circles spell LILY SAVAGE, the name of *Blankety Blank* host Paul O'Grady's drag alter ego.

Page 27: RuPaul's Drag Race
Snatch Match
In the order given in the left-hand column, the drag queens and their chosen celebrities are as follows, with the number indicating the correct image:
Baga Chipz/Margaret Thatcher (1)
Bimini Bon Boulash/Katie Price (2)
Ella Vaday/Nigella Lawson (3)
Lawrence Chaney/Miriam Margolyes (4)
Scarlett Harlett/Macaulay Culkin (5)
The Vivienne/Donald Trump (6)

Lip-Synch
HALLUCINATE + VANITY MILAN
CALL MY NAME + CHERYL HOLE
WOULD I LIE TO YOU + VINEGAR STROKES
TOUCH ME + TIA KOFI

Page 29: Strictly Come Dancing
Winner, Winner
In the order given, the dancers and dances are:
1. Natasha Kaplinsky + quickstep
2. Darren Gough + Argentine tango
3. Mark Ramprakash + American smooth
4. Alesha Dixon + foxtrot
5. Louis Smith + samba
6. Abbey Clancy + cha-cha-cha
7. Stacey Dooley + paso doble
8. Kelvin Fletcher + Viennese waltz

Scores on the Doors
A. Craig Revel Horwood (2)
B. Len Goodman (7)
C. Arlene Phillips (5)
D. Alesha Dixon (8)
E. Darcey Bussell (6)
F. Shirley Ballas (4)
G. Motsi Mabuse (9)
H. Anton Du Beke (3)
I. Bruno Tonioli (10), so he has the highest score

Page 31: Dragons' Den
Torn to Shreds
BrewDog (craft beer); Cup-a-wine (portable pre-filled wine glasses); Destination (Hamley's bestselling board game); Tangle Teezer (hairbrush); Trunki (ride-on suitcases for children)

A Slice of the Pie
AUTOSAFE; EGGXACTLY; HAMFATTER; HUNGRYHOUSE; IGLOO; KIDDIMOTO; LUMACOUSTICS; NIMBLE; OCUSHIELD; REMPODS; SEABUNG; SLINKS; SPOON; UMBROLLY

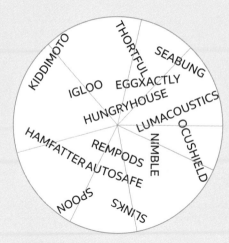

Slippery Slope
- HIRED
- PAIRED
- CHAIRED
- INSPIRED
- BACKFIRED
- ACQUIRED
- RETIRED
- SPIRED
- FIRED

CHAPTER 2: DRAMA

Page 39: Costume Drama
The Chronology of Costume
In order from left to right, top to bottom, the images are taken from the following programmes:
Upstairs, Downstairs (1930s)
Life on Mars (1970s)
Call the Midwife (1950s/1960s)
Poldark (1780s)
Gentleman Jack (1830s)
Wolf Hall (1520s/1530s)
I, Claudius (24BC–54CE)
Ashes to Ashes (1980s)
North and South (1850s)

The letters, when arranged in chronological order of the images, spell ALEX DRAKE, the name of the protagonist in *Ashes to Ashes*.

The Art and the Artist
1. J.B. PRIESTLEY + BUSTLE
2. Henry FIELDING + DOUBLET
3. Flora THOMPSON + CORSET
4. Gustave FLAUBERT + BONNET
5. George Bernard SHAW + PETTICOAT
6. Thomas HARDY + BREECHES
7. Oscar WILDE + CHEMISE
8. Victor HUGO + BODICE

Page 41: *Pride and Prejudice*
The Perfect Match
1. Elizabeth
2. Elizabeth
3. Darcy
4. Elizabeth
5. Darcy
6. Darcy
7. Elizabeth
8. Darcy
9. Darcy

Page 33: *Top Gear*
The Mysterious Stig

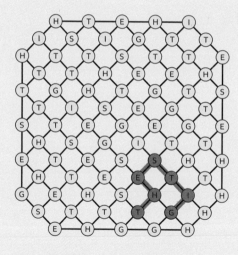

Drivers and Rides
1. (Daniel) RICCIARDO + CHEVROLET
2. (Lewis) HAMILTON + MERCEDES
3. (Sebastian) VETTEL + NISSAN
4. (Rubens) BARRICHELLO + LAMBORGHINI
5. (Jenson) BUTTON + TOYOTA
6. (Kimi) RAIKKONEN + ALFA ROMEO
7. (Damon) HILL + FORD
8. (Michael) SCHUMACHER + VOLKSWAGEN

Page 35: *The Apprentice*
Sport Relief
1. (Claire) BALDING + ARCHERY
2. (Nick) HANCOCK + FENCING
3. (Louise) REDKNAPP + FOOTBALL
4. (Phil) TUFNELL + SAILING

Face to Face

The couples are as follows, with their number labels indicating their position when read from left to right, top to bottom:

Charles Bingley (8) and Jane Bennet (5);
with a shift of 3
Lydia Bennet (1) and George Wickham (3);
with a shift of 2
Fitzwilliam Darcy (2) and Elizabeth Bennet (5);
with a shift of 4
Charlotte Lucas (4) and William Collins (7);
with a shift of 1

Page 43: Landmark Drama
Our Friends in the North

1. Daniel Craig: *Copenhagen*, *Saint-Ex*
2. Christopher Eccleston: *Doctor Who*, *The A Word*
3. Mark Strong: *The Long Firm*, *Who Do You Think You Are?* (narrator)
4. Gina McKee: *Bodyguard*, *The Silence*

Talking Heads

1. A Woman of No IMPORTANCE
2. A Chip in the SUGAR
3. A Lady of LETTERS
4. Bed Among the LENTILS
5. Her Big CHANCE
6. A Cream Cracker Under the SETTEE
7. Miss Fozzard Finds Her FEET
8. The Hand of GOD
9. Playing SANDWICHES
10. The Outside DOG
11. Nights in the Gardens of SPAIN
12. Waiting for the TELEGRAM
13. An Ordinary WOMAN
14. The SHRINE

Page 45: *Play for Today*
Play for Yesterday

The highlighted letters are E, C, W, S, E, N, R, O and T, which can be rearranged to spell SCREEN TWO.

Page 47: *Edge of Darkness*
Hiding in the Shadows

1. COLD: to give COMMON COLD and COLD FRAME
2. WAR: to give CIVIL WAR and WAR ZONE
3. HOT: to give PIPING HOT and HOT TICKET
4. CELL: to give BRAIN CELL and CELL BLOCK
5. COVER: to give BREAK COVER and COVER STORY
6. UP: to give BUCKLE UP and UP STICKS

The centre words read 'Cold War hot cell cover up', a central plot point of the show.

Uncovered, Unfortunately

The word PLUTONIUM is revealed. The solutions are:
PINPOINT; INTUITION; LIMIT; POLLUTION

Page 49: *I May Destroy You*
Character Fit

David – the name of the show's main antagonist – is the only name that does not fit into the grid. The other names fit as follows:

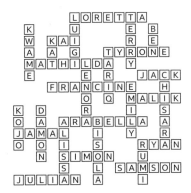

Social Muddle

In the order they appear in the puzzle, the social media platforms and their extra letters are:

Facebook + T
Instagram + W
Snapchat + I
TikTok + T
Pinterest + T
WhatsApp + E
YouTube + R

The extra channel is therefore Twitter.

Page 51: The Crime Drama
Crime Scenes

1. *Bergerac* – JERSEY
2. *Happy Valley* – WEST YORKSHIRE
3. *Hidden* – SNOWDONIA
4. *Hope Street* – NORTHERN IRELAND
5. *Luther* – LONDON
6. *Peaky Blinders* – BIRMINGHAM
7. *Silent Witness* – CAMBRIDGE
8. *The Missing* – FRANCE
9. *Vigil* – SUBMARINE

Page 53: *Peaky Blinders*
Family Ties

1. Martha Strong
2. Arthur Shelby Jr
3. Elizabeth Shelby
4. Arthur Shelby Jr
5. Linda Shelby
6. Grace Burgess
7. Tommy Shelby
8. Lizzie Stark
9. John Shelby
10. Esme Lee
11. Ada Shelby
12. Freddie Thorne
13. Finn Shelby
14. Michael Gray
15. Gina Gray
16. Billy Shelby
17. Charles Shelby
18. Ruby Shelby
19. Karl Thorne

Target Practice

The occupation that uses all the letters is
BOOKMAKER
AMOK; KABOOM; ROB; BROKE; MOB; ROAM

Page 55: Action, Myth, Adventure
Other-Worldly Experiences

1. Camelot – *Merlin*
2. Discworld – *Eric*
3. Lower Earth – *ElvenQuest*
4. Northumbria – *Wolfblood*
5. Otherworld – *Pilgrim*
6. Oxford – *His Dark Materials*
7. South Wales – *Wizards vs Aliens*
8. Yorkshire – *The Railway Children*

The Radio 4 shows are *ElvenQuest*, *Eric* and *Pilgrim*.

Legendary Figures

From top to bottom, the names of the characters are as follows:

Gaius; Morgana; Guinevere; Merlin; Uther; Arthur
Gaius is the only name not to appear in Arthurian legend.

Page 57: *The Chronicles of Narnia*
The Chronicles of Narnia

1. *The Lion, the Witch and the Wardrobe*
2. *Prince Caspian*
3. *The Voyage of the Dawn Treader*
4. *The Silver Chair*
5. *The Horse and His Boy*
6. *The Magician's Nephew*
7. *The Last Battle*

Circular Tales

1. Peter
2. Susan
3. Aslan
4. Witch
5. Table
6. Kirke

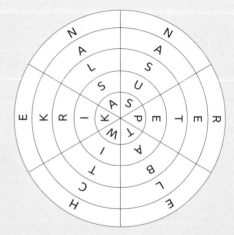

Page 59: Spies and Spooks
Following Villanelle
To find the hidden cities, read down while crossing out letters when used. From left to right across the top row, reading downwards, you can find: VIENNA; LONDON; PARIS; BERLIN; MOSCOW; AMSTERDAM; ROME; BARCELONA; ABERDEEN

Chain Reaction
The pyramids can be completed as follows, with the spies highlighted:
1. SPY SPRY PREYS REPAYS PLAYERS SPARSELY
2. TEN NEAT AGENT MAGNET GARMENT ARGUMENT
3. ELM MOLE MOTEL MOLEST MOTTLES LEFTMOST
4. SAT EAST ASSET STATES ATTESTS ASTUTEST

Page 61: *Tinker Tailor Soldier Spy*
Last Man Standing

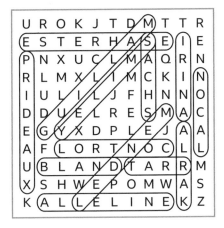

The only name not to appear is HAYDON – the name of the mole in *Tinker Tailor Soldier Spy*.

The Spy Ring
AGENT; MOLE; PLANT; SLEEPER; SPOOK

Page 63: Science Fiction
The BBC's Guide to the Galaxy
The programme names each contain a hidden 'up', 'down', 'left' or 'right':
1. *Coupling*
2. *My Left Nut*
3. *Love Soup*
4. *Puppy Love*
5. *Pinwright's Progress*
6. *The Wright Way*
7. *Down to Earth*
8. *The Kids Are All Right*

9. *RuPaul's Drag Race UK*
10. *Upstart Crow*
11. *Wright Around the World*
12. *Two Doors Down*
13. *Watership Down*

The path created by following these instructions spells out MOSTLY HARMLESS

Radio Drama
The corresponding original titles are as follows:
A Dream of Armageddon (A Dram of Armaddon)
In the Abyss (In T Aby)
The Sea Raiders (T a Raidr)
The War of the Worlds (T ar of t ord)
The Door in the Wall (T Door in t a)
The First Men in the Moon (T Firt Mn in t Moon)
The New Accelerator (T N Accrator)
The Treasure in the Forest (T Traur in t For)

Page 65: *Doctor Who*
Hidden Villain
The names can be filled in as follows, revealing the name CASSANDRA:

Restoring Order

The missing companion is JACK HARKNESS. Reading from top to bottom, left to right, the doctors and their corresponding actors are as follows (numbers in brackets denote chronology):

Sylvester McCoy (7th)
Peter Capaldi (12th)
Jodie Whittaker (13th)
Paul McGann (8th)
Tom Baker (4th)
Christopher Eccleston (9th)
Patrick Troughton (2nd)
William Hartnell (1st)
Colin Baker (6th)
Jon Pertwee (3rd)
Matt Smith (11th)
David Tennant (10th)
Peter Davison (5th)

Page 67: Radiophonic Workshop
Cut the Tape

The crossed-out letters spell WOBBULATOR:

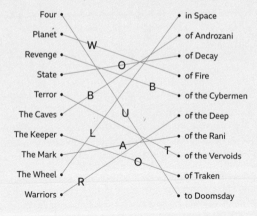

Four •	• in Space
Planet •	• of Androzani
Revenge •	• of Decay
State •	• of Fire
Terror •	• of the Cybermen
The Caves •	• of the Deep
The Keeper •	• of the Rani
The Mark •	• of the Vervoids
The Wheel •	• of Traken
Warriors •	• to Doomsday

Words and Waves

BELLS
BOTTLES
GRAVEL
VOICE
KEYS
COMBS

Page 69: BBC Film
Adapted Adaptations

1. I CAPTURE THE CASTLE by Dodie Smith
2. BRIGHTON ROCK by Graham Greene
3. FAR FROM THE MADDING CROWD by Thomas Hardy
4. A LONG WAY DOWN by Nick Hornby
5. JANE EYRE by Charlotte Brontë
6. THE LADY IN THE VAN by Alan Bennett
7. THE MEN WHO STARE AT GOATS by Jon Ronson
8. THE POWER OF THE DOG by Thomas Savage

The Line-Up

1. FREESTYLE – Two would-be students fall in love over basketball lessons, despite external efforts to keep them apart, starring Arinzé Kene
2. BROOKLYN – A young Irish woman struggles to adapt to life on both sides of the Atlantic, starring Saoirse Ronan
3. LILTING – A mother grieves for her son alongside his lover, though they have no common language, starring Ben Whishaw
4. IRIS – The real-life story of a writer with Alzheimer's and her husband, starring Judi Dench and Jim Broadbent
5. CORIOLANUS – Adaptation of one of Shakespeare's tragedies, starring Ralph Fiennes
6. MISBEHAVIOUR – A group of women seek to interrupt the 1970 Miss World competition, starring Keira Knightley
7. BREATHE – A young man paralyzed by polio rebuilds his life with the help of his wife, starring Claire Foy and Andrew Garfield

When arranged into alphabetical order, the first letters spell BBC FILM.

CHAPTER 3: COMEDY

Page 73: Classic Comedy
On the Double
The highlighted letters spell MONTY PYTHON:

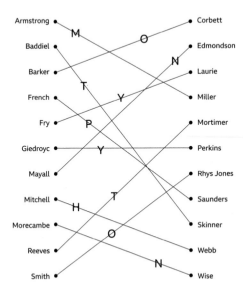

Armstrong • — • Corbett
Baddiel • — • Edmondson
Barker • — • Laurie
French • — • Miller
Fry • — • Mortimer
Giedroyc • — • Perkins
Mayall • — • Rhys Jones
Mitchell • — • Saunders
Morecambe • — • Skinner
Reeves • — • Webb
Smith • — • Wise

M O N T Y P Y T H Ø N

First Name Basis
The first names match as follows:
• Alexander Armstrong and Ben Miller
• David Baddiel and Frank Skinner
• David Mitchell and Robert Webb
• Dawn French and Jennifer Saunders
• Eric Morecambe and Ernie Wise
• Mel Smith and Griff Rhys Jones
• Mel Giedroyc and Sue Perkins
• Rik Mayall and Ade Edmondson
• Ronnie Barker and Ronnie Corbett
• Stephen Fry and Hugh Laurie
• Vic Reeves and Bob Mortimer

Page 75: *Dad's Army*
Under Fire
1. BITE THE BULLET
2. LOST THE BATTLE BUT WON THE WAR
3. LOOSE CANNON
4. FIGHT FIRE WITH FIRE
5. TAKE THE FLAK
6. YOU AND WHOSE ARMY

The Line-Up
From left to right the characters are:
1. Private Godfrey
2. Lance Corporal Jones
3. Captain Mainwaring
4. Private Pike
5. Private Frazer
6. Sergeant Wilson

And the person missing from the photo is
7. Private Walker

Enter the letter correctly and your phrase will be IN ORDER.

Page 77: Sitcoms
Blackadder Through the Ages
1. *Blackadder the Third* – Regency
2. *Blackadder Goes Forth* – World War I
3. *Blackadder II* – Elizabethan
4. *The Black Adder* – Middle Ages

Fabulously Absolute
The revealed name is ELTON JOHN – who Jennifer Saunders' character Edina insulted in the episode 'Schmoozin'.

E	J	H	A	T	O	N	S	L
S	L	O	N	J	E	A	T	H
A	N	T	L	H	S	J	E	O
N	T	S	O	A	L	H	J	E
H	A	J	E	N	T	L	O	S
O	E	L	H	S	J	T	N	A
L	S	N	T	E	H	O	A	J
J	O	A	S	L	N	E	H	T
T	H	E	J	O	A	S	L	N

Page 79: *Fawlty Towers*
Worst Flaw Yet
1. A Touch of Class
2. The Builders
3. The Wedding Party
4. The Hotel Inspectors
5. Gourmet Night
6. The Germans
7. Communication Problems
8. The Psychiatrist
9. Waldorf Salad
10. The Kipper and the Corpse
11. The Anniversary
12. Basil the Rat

Quite Quotable
1. 'Don't mention the war.' (The Germans)
2. 'If you don't like duck . . . then you're rather stuck.' (Gourmet Night)
3. 'I'll put an ad in the papers: "Wanted, kind home for enormous savage rodent. Answers to the name of Sybil." ' (Basil the Rat)
4. 'I'm so sorry, I'm afraid the dining room door seems to have disappeared.' (The Builders)
5. 'Now, please, please, try to understand before one of us dies.' (Communication Problems)
6. 'There's enough there for an entire convention.' (The Psychiatrist)
7. 'Oh, spiffing. Absolutely spiffing. Well done. Two dead, twenty-five to go.' (The Kipper and the Corpse)
8. 'Yes, it's a traditional old English thing. It's apples, grapefruit and potatoes in a mayonnaise sauce.' (Waldorf Salad)

Page 81: Alternative Comedy
French and Saunders
1. *Beauty and the Beast* (film)
2. *Modern Mother and Daughter* (sketch)
3. *Pride and Prejudice* (book and TV series)
4. *Rosemary and Thyme* (TV series)
5. The Mamas and The Papas (band)
6. *The Quick and the Dead* (film)
7. *Thelma and Louise* (film)

No Relation
1. Alive and well
2. Back and forth
3. Bells and whistles
4. Bits and bobs
5. Fine and dandy
6. This and that
7. Thick and fast
8. Vim and vigour
9. Warts and all
10. Well and good

Page 83: *Monty Python's Flying Circus*
Unexpected Ending
1. Dead Parrot
2. Dirty Fork
3. Fish License
4. Marriage Guidance Counsellor
5. Seduced Milkmen
6. The Funniest Joke in the World
7. The Lumberjack Song
8. The Ministry of Silly Walks
9. The Spanish Inquisition

The Man Who Speaks in Anagrams
Macbeth; *Othello*; *Coriolanus*; *Cymbeline*; Much Ado About *Nothing*; *Pericles*; *Measure* for Measure; The *Merchant* of Venice; The *Tempest*; The Two Gentlemen of *Verona*; The Winter's *Tale*; *Hamlet*; Timon of *Athens*

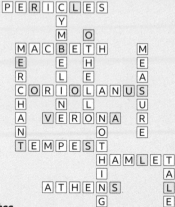

Page 85: *Fleabag*
What's in a Name?
The names can be unscrambled as follows:
1. JAKE + G
2. CLAIRE + U
3. MARTIN + I
4. HARRY + N
5. FLEABAG + E
6. GODMOTHER + A
7. DAD + P
8. BOO + I
9. THE PRIEST + G
Hilary's characteristic is that she is a pet GUINEA PIG.

Find the Statue
The stolen statues can be found in the following places:

<table>
<tr><td>♟</td><td>2</td><td>♟</td><td>2</td><td>1</td></tr>
<tr><td></td><td>3</td><td></td><td>2</td><td>♟</td></tr>
<tr><td>1</td><td>♟</td><td></td><td>2</td><td></td></tr>
<tr><td>2</td><td></td><td>♟</td><td></td><td>1</td></tr>
<tr><td>♟</td><td>2</td><td>2</td><td>♟</td><td>1</td></tr>
</table>

Page 85: *The Office*
Making Cuts
APPRAISALS; DOWNSIZE; INTERVIEW; JUDGEMENT; MERGER; MOTIVATION; PARTY; TRAINING

REDUNDANCY has been split into four parts – and is therefore the only word not to be an episode title.

Employee of the Month
DAVID BRENT: GENERAL MANAGER
TIM CANTERBURY: SALES REPRESENTATIVE
DAWN TINSLEY: COMPANY RECEPTIONIST
RICKY HOWARD: OFFICE TEMP
JENNIFER TAYLOR-CLARKE: HEAD OFFICE
DONNA: WORK EXPERIENCE

Page 89: Comic Relief
Red Nose Day
1. *Beauty and the Beast*
2. *Doctor Who*
3. *Line of Duty*
4. *The Vicar of Dibley*
5. *University Challenge*
6. *Dragons' Den*
7. *Little Britain*

Barely Recognizable
'Uptown Downstairs Abbey' – *A Downton Abbey* Parody
'Spider-Plant Man' – *A Spider-Man* Parody

Potter Parody
1. Ronnie Corbett (one of The Two Ronnies) as Hagrid
2. Dawn French as Harry Potter
3. Jennifer Saunders (Edina in *Absolutely Fabulous*) as Ron Weasley
4. Alison Steadman (Gavin's Mum in *Gavin and Stacey*) as Professor McGonagall

Basil Brush was Dobby the House Elf.

Page 91: Radio Comedy
Ladies of Letters
1. Vera	2. Anthony
3. Howard	4. ?
5. Karen	6. St John
7. Flo	8. Nelson
9. Millie	10. Irene
11. ?	12. Lesley
13. Brian	14. Margaret
15. Christopher	16. Michaela
17. Cheryl-Marie	18. Bubbles
19. Sophie-Irene	20. Little Christopher
21. Tommy	

Needle in a Haystack
The show's title is THE PIN; other words include hen, nip, pen, pent, pine, pint and then.

Page 93: The Hitchhiker's Guide
The Hitchhiker's Journey

64	63	59	58	36	35	42	43
62	60	57	32	34	37	44	41
61	55	56	33	31	45	38	40
53	54	50	48	46	30	24	39
52	51	49	47	29	28	25	23
2	1	10	12	27	26	22	21
5	3	9	11	13	17	18	20
4	6	7	8	14	15	16	19

Spinning Around
JONES (that is, Simon Jones); FROOD; TOWEL; BANJO; NOVEL; EARTH

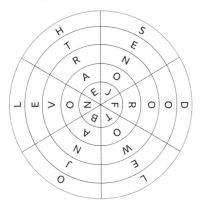

Page 95: *Hancock's Half Hour*
Hancock's Second Half

(crossword grid solution) with answers including: CHRISTMAS; CONTEST; DOG; MATCH; POLICY; BAR; HORSE; SHAME; MONEY; GAME; JEWELS; CHAMPION; SANTA; TOWN; SERIES

CHAPTER 4: SOAP OPERA

Page 99: BBC Soaps
Soaps and Water
From top to bottom, left to right, the title cards are as follows:
EastEnders; *River City*; *Triangle*; *Eldorado*; *Howard's Way*; *Rownd a Rownd* (a Welsh-language show distributed by the BBC)

Compact
1. DOWN THE HATCH
2. MOMENT OF TRUTH
3. THE MAN FOR THE JOB
4. COMINGS AND GOINGS
5. RIDING FOR A FALL
6. ALL THAT JAZZ
7. BUSINESS AS USUAL
8. SHOCK TACTICS
9. SENT TO COVENTRY
10. LOVE YOU AND LEAVE YOU
11. THE TRUTH WILL OUT

Page 99: *EastEnders*
Families on the Square
The characters are:
- Ian BEALE
- Martin FOWLER
- Max BRANNING
- Stacey SLATER
- Peggy MITCHELL
- Pat BUTCHER
- Shabnam MASOOD
- Mick CARTER
- Dot COTTON
- Den WATTS

☆	A	L	E	F	R	B	R
B	E	C	T	O	E	N	A
L	E	H	I	W	L	N	I
L	T	C	M	R	E	T	N
B	U	H	E	R	C	A	G
M	R	E	T	T	O	L	S
A	O	D	R	T	W	A	S
S	O	C	A	O	N	T	T

Page 103: *Casualty*
Hiding in Plain Sight
1. Anita Dobson
2. Celia Imrie
3. David Walliams
4. Martin Freeman
5. Helen Baxendale
6. Tom Hiddleston
7. Andrew Sachs
8. Kate Winslet
9. Prunella Scales
10. Christopher Eccleston
11. Orlando Bloom

Staff List
Connie Beauchamp (Clinical Lead)
Charlie Fairhead (Emergency Nurse)
Dylan Keogh (Consultant)
Ethan Hardy (Registrar)
Iain Dean (Paramedic)
Jade Lovall (Staff Nurse)
Jan Jenning (Duty Manager)
Marty Kirkby (Student Nurse)
Rash Masum (Junior Doctor)

Page 105: *The Archers*
Home Sweet Home
The fictional locations are:
Ambridge (the main village)
Borchester (Borsetshire's county town)
Borsetshire (the county containing Ambridge)
Brookfield (the farm owned by the Archer family)
Felpersham (the nearest city to Ambridge)
Home Farm (the farm owned by the Aldridge family)
Lower Loxley Hall (the stately home owned by the Pargetter family)
Loxley Barrett (another fictional village)

Penny Hassett (another fictional village)
The Bull (the pub in Ambridge)

The locations that do not appear in *The Archers* are connected as follows:
Barwick Green is the name of the opening theme
Cutnall Green – a real village – is said to have been the basis for Ambridge
Hanbury – a real village – houses a church that is used as a stand-in location
Inkberrow – a real village – houses a pub on which The Bull is modelled

Hidden Talents
From left to right, the images are:
- Princess Margaret (appeared in an episode commemorating the NSPCC)
- Judi Dench (appeared in the 10,000thh episode as a character who has previously always been silent)
- John Peel (appeared as themselves, in a 'radio on the radio')
- Alan Titchmarsh (judged entries from the villagers of Ambridge in the National Gardens Scheme)
- Chris Moyles (appeared in The Bull as a suspected 'mystery judge' for a 'Pub of the Year' competition)
- Terry Wogan (appeared as themselves, prompting a previously silent character to break their silence)
- Camilla, Duchess of Cornwall (appeared in association with the National Osteoporosis Society, of which they are a patron)
- Bradley Wiggins (presented prizes at an Ambridge Sport Relief contest)

CHAPTER 5: SPORT

Page 109: Sports Regulars
Game Set Match

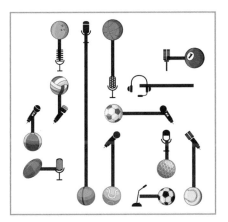

Sporting Chances
1. Gary Lineker: *Match of the Day*
2. Sue Barker: *Today at Wimbledon*
3. Phil Tufnell: *Test Match Special*
4. Chemmy Alcott: *Ski Sunday*

Page 111: *Match of the Day*
Keepy-Uppy
Arsenal – Thierry Henry – Highbury – 8th
Chelsea – Frank Lampard – Stamford Bridge – 4th
Everton – Dixie Dean – Goodison Park – 10th
Liverpool – Ian Rush – Anfield – 3rd
Manchester United – Wayne Rooney – Old Trafford – 2nd
Tottenham Hotspur – Jimmy Greaves – White Hart Lane – 7th

On the Ball
Bale; Table; Fibulae; Blue; Fuel; Beautiful – since football is often described as 'the beautiful game'.

Page 113: Live Sports Coverage
Some Questions of Sport
1. Putney Bridge and Chiswick Bridge
2. Nicola Adams
3. 2013
4. Jofra Archer
5. Jonny Wilkinson
6. Bradley Wiggins
7. Two
8. Kelly Holmes
9. 2017–2020
10. They have all won gold medals at the Summer Olympics or Paralympics. The athletes are:
a. Jessica Ennis-Hill
b. Ellie Simmonds
c. Rebecca Adlington
d. Sarah Storey

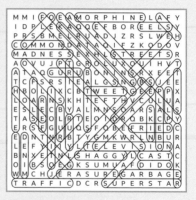

Page 117: *Top of the Pops*
Change of Key

Each name has been disguised by changing all of the letters that are also musical notes into the 'note' that comes before it. So, A has been changed to G; B has been changed to A; and so on until G becomes F. The revealed names and facts are, in the order given:

1. CLIFF RICHARD (B)
2. 'MAGGIE MAY' (A)
3. SERGE GAINSBOURG (F)
4. GREEN DAY (C)
5. THE BEATLES (D)
6. OASIS (E)

Missing Notes

'(Everything I Do) I Do It For You' by Bryan Adams
'Bohemian Rhapsody' by Queen
'Do You Really Want to Hurt Me' by Culture Club
'Love is All Around' by Wet Wet Wet
'Relax' by Frankie Goes to Hollywood
'You're the First, the Last, My Everything' by Barry White

As of the start of 2022, Bryan Adams' song '(Everything I Do) I Do It For You' still holds the record for most consecutive weeks spent as the UK's No.1.

Page 119: *Later. . . with Jools Holland*
Emerging Artists

In the given order, the clued artists are: Cast; Belly; Elbow; Skin; Cracker; Tweet; Battles; Fried; Erasure; Oasis; Tricky; Incognito; Superstar; Ash; Common; Shaggy; Hole; Embrace; Placebo; Earthling; Madness; Denim; Beirut; Klaxons; Seal; Dido; Editors; Oslo; Reef; Feeder; Morphine; Aqualung; Pulp; Ruby; Streets; Garbage; Blur; Eels; Guru; Athlete; Jellyfish; Jet; Pretenders; Doves; Texas; Traffic; Suede; Sting; Television; Foals

They can be found in the grid as follows:

Page 121: BBC Proms
Last Night at the Proms

'JERUSALEM' + TIMPANI
'AULD LANG SYNE' + CLARINET
'LAND OF HOPE AND GLORY' + TROMBONE
'FANTASIA ON BRITISH SEA SONGS' + XYLOPHONE
'RULE, BRITANNIA!' + GLOCKENSPIEL
'GOD SAVE THE QUEEN' + BASSOON

True and False

A. FALSE: While smoking and eating were once permitted, it is now illegal to smoke at The Proms
B. TRUE
C. TRUE
D. FALSE: It is true, however, that a French orchestra once played a Daft Punk piece as an encore
E. FALSE: Marin Alsop became the first female Last Night conductor in 2013
F. FALSE: The Proms carried on throughout both world wars
G. TRUE

Page 123: Live Aid
Last Man Singing

Paul McCartney (who performed with Geldof, Bowie, Alison Moyet and Pete Townsend)

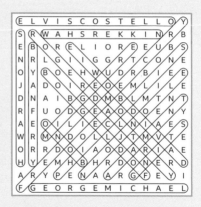

All In Order

The order of appearance was as follows:
Status Quo; Boomtown Rats; Spandau Ballet; Elvis Costello; Sade; Dire Straits; Queen; The Who

Page 125: Disc Jockeys
The Face Behind the Mic

Top to bottom, left to right, the images show the following DJs, with the added numbers giving the order of their tenure as Breakfast presenter:

- Sara Cox (8)
- Tony Blackburn (1)
- Simon Mayo (6)
- Zoe Ball (7)
- Noel Edmonds (2)
- Greg James (11)
- Nick Grimshaw (10)
- Mike Read (4)
- Dave Lee Travis (3)
- Mike Smith (5)
- Chris Moyles (9)

When arranged in the numerical order shown above, the added letters spell NIGHTINGALE – the surname of Annie Nightingale, the first female BBC DJ.

CHAPTER 7: FACTUAL

Page 129: Landmark Factual Shows
The Ascent of Man

The lines reveal ANTHONY HOPKINS:

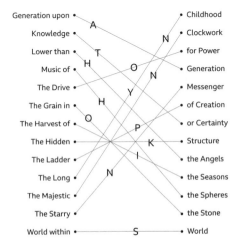

The Shock of the New

The artwork is *Guernica*, by Pablo Picasso.
Words that can be found include acre, air, anger, arc, arcing, are, argue, auger, cagier, cairn, car, care, caring, cigar, crag, crane, cringe, cur, cure, curie, curing, ear, earn, ecru, era, erg, gear, grace, grain, grin, incur, inure, ire, nacre, near, nicer, race, racing, rag, rage, rain, ran, rang, range, regain, reign, rein, rice, rig, ring, rue, rug, ruin, ruing, run, rune, rung, urge, uric and urn.

Page 131: *Mastermind*
I've Started, So I'll Finish

Abraham LINCOLN
Academy AWARDS
Doctor WHO
Édith PIAF
Empress LIVIA
Father TED
Francis DRAKE
Grand OPERA
Nancy ASTOR
Olympic FENCING
Otis REDDING
Romanov DYNASTY
Shakespeare's PLAYS
Solar SYSTEM
Westminster ABBEY

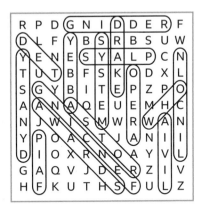

Specialist Subject: The BBC

1. 1985
2. Parrot
3. *Jools' Annual Hootenanny*
4. Fabergé
5. The Royal Albert Hall
6. Shelby
7. Supermarine Spitfire
8. Bruce Forsythe
9. The Queen Victoria
10. Borsetshire

Page 133: *Only Connect*

Connections

1) Things found in a PAC-MAN game
2) LEGO themes
3) Parts of a piano
4) Maths terms

Connecting Wall

Parts of a plant: Flower; Leaf; Stalk; Root

Terms used in tennis: Ace; Seed; Slice; Baseline

Synonyms for having a favourable position: Advantage; Superiority; Edge; Lead

Words that are also a word when written backwards: Desserts (stressed); Draw (ward); Bulb (blub); Tuber (rebut)

Missing Vowels

1) Beethoven; Elgar; Dvorak; Cage
2) Judo; Ice Hockey; Archery; Ultimate Frisbee

Page 135: Michael Palin's Travels

Around the World in 80 Steps

The names can be found in the grid in the following order:

United Kingdom; France; Austria; Italy; Greece; Egypt; Qatar; Singapore; China; Japan; India – which is in the wrong location, as it was visited between Qatar and Singapore in the programme

Full Circle

Reading from left to right, top to bottom, countries and their additional letters are:

- Colombia + A
- Philippines + A
- South Korea + C
- Indonesia + N
- Bolivia + D
- Australia + A

In the show, the countries were visited in the following order: South Korea, Philippines, Indonesia, Australia, Bolivia, Colombia – giving the final country name CANADA from the extracted letters.

Page 137: *Great Railway Journeys*

Here to There

The places can be paired as follows, in the order of the left column as given:

- Calcutta to Rajasthan: adjacent letter pairs swapped (ACCLTUAT – ARAJTSAHN)
- Aleppo to Aqaba: letters arranged into alphabetical order (AELOPP – AAABQ)
- Derry to Kerry: letters shifted one place forward in the alphabet (EFSSZ – LFSSZ)
- Granada to Salamanca: vowels removed (GRND – SLMNC)
- Tokyo to Kagoshima: first and second part of each name swapped (KYOTO – SHIMAKAGO)
- London to Arcadia: first and final letters removed (ONDO – RCADI)
- Singapore to Bangkok: letters in reverse alphabetical order (SRPONIGEA – ONKKGBA)

Crewe to Crewe

The loop reveals the name VICTORIA WOOD. As an extra hint, the un-crossed letters read 'UNUSED LETTERS' when read in usual reading order.

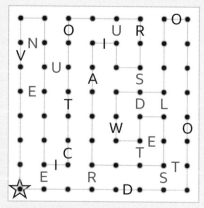

Page 139: *Antiques Roadshow*

Collector's Edition

£20,000: CHARLOTTE BRONTË mourning ring

£25,000: BEATRIX POTTER first editions

£30,000: WILLIAM SHAKESPEARE review notebook

£50,000: STAR WARS prop helmet

£400,000: GEORGE HARRISON's fretless guitar

£1,000,000: FABERGÉ pear blossom

Location, Location

The restored 'castle' locations are as follows:
Bolsover Castle; Barnard Castle; Castle Howard; Hever Castle; Kendal Castle; Alnwick Castle; Pembroke Castle; Cardiff Castle; Auckland Castle

Page 141: *The Sky at Night*
The Natural Order

1. Royal Observatory, Greenwich, founded (1675)
2. Edmond Halley first predicts the appearance of the periodical comet (1705)
3. The planet Uranus is discovered (1781)
4. Sputnik 1 is launched by the USSR (1957)
5. NASA founded (1958)
6. Apollo 11 astronauts are the first to walk on the moon (1969)
7. Hubble Space Telescope launched (1990)
8. First long-term residents arrive at the International Space Station (2000)
9. Pluto reclassified as a dwarf planet (2006)
10. Curiosity rover lands on Mars (2012)

Obscured Objects

Sun; Black Hole; Mars; Comet; Venus
The incorrect letters spell out MOORE, the surname of *The Sky at Night*'s longest-standing presenter

Astronomy Quiz

1. Uranus; 2. Sirius; 3. Asteroid; 4. Polaris; 5. Helen Sharman

Page 143: *Horizon*
A Question of Questions

1. Are We Alone in the UNIVERSE?
2. Are We Still EVOLVING?
3. Can VENICE Survive?
4. Can We Make a STAR on Earth?
5. Could FISH Make My Child Smart?
6. Did COOKING Make Us Human?
7. Did DARWIN Get It Wrong?
8. Do COWS Make You Mad?
9. Do We Really Need the RAILWAYS?
10. Do You Dig National PARKS?
11. How Long is a Piece of STRING?
12. How Much Do You SMELL?
13. How Safe is SURGERY?
14. Should We Close Our ZOOS?
15. So You Want to Be an INVENTOR?
16. What Makes an ANIMAL Smart?
17. What Really Killed the DINOSAURS?
18. What's Killing Our BEES?
19. What's Wrong with the SUN?
20. Where Must the MONEY Go?
21. Who Will Deliver Your BABY?

Note that all the leftover letters consist purely of letters from 'HORIZON':

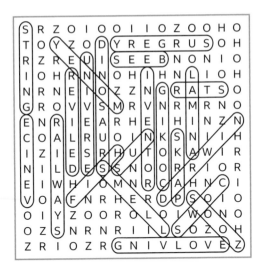

Page 145: The Open University
Irregular Programming

Maths Terms	Plant Parts	Body Parts	Greek Myth
Area	Anther	Digit	Hercules
Circumference	Petal	Hand	Iris
Percentage	Sepal	Neck	Venus
Root	Stamen	Palm	Zeus

Honorary Graduates

1. Quentin Blake
   (*The Drawing of My Life*)
2. David Attenborough
   (*Blue Planet II*)
3. Mary Beard
   (*Julius Caesar Revealed*)
4. Jeremy Paxman
   (*University Challenge*)

Page 147: *Desert Island Discs*
Frequent Castaway
David Attenborough. The clues can be solved as follows:

E	N	D	E	A	R	I	N	G

A	D	O	R	E	D

A	D	V	E	N	T	U	R	E	R

D	A	V	I	D		A	T	T	E	N	B	O	R	O	U	G	H

1	2	3	4	5	6	7	8	9	10	11	12	13
E	B	N	D	I	U	A	G	R	V	H	T	O

Play It Again
The Beatles
Gather = 'Come Together'
Our closest star is arriving = 'Here Comes the Sun'
Allow it to exist = 'Let It Be'
Only feelings of adoration are required = 'All You Need Is Love'
Turdus merula = 'Blackbird'
During the soft lachrymation of my six-stringed instrument = 'While My Guitar Gently Weeps'
Alongside small amounts of assistance from my companions = 'With A Little Help from My Friends'
Rotate and yell = 'Twist and Shout'
Pastures of red, seeded fruits indefinitely = 'Strawberry Fields Forever'
The day immediately preceding today = 'Yesterday'

Page 149: *Woman's Hour*
The First Hours
1. Cookery
2. Hairdressing
3. Childcare
4. Fashion

The quote is: 'Believe that women are interested in everything – absolutely everything.'

Faces on the Radio
Looking at the images from left to right, top to bottom, the guest editors are as follows:
- Kim Cattrall (5)
- Dame Kelly Holmes (2)
- Ellie Simmonds (4)
- J.K. Rowling (6)
- Jacqueline Wilson (1)
- Zawe Ashton (3)

Page 151: *Tomorrow's World*
They Need No Introduction
The restored objects are as follows:
- ARTIFICIAL GRASS
- ELECTRONIC VIDEO RECORDER
- IN-VITRO FERTILIZATION
- CONCORDE
- TELETEXT
- SYNTHESIZER
- CAMCORDER
- AERIAL MAPPING

Future Findings
The solutions can be found in the following order in the grid:
SNOOKER (the sport played by Hissing Sid)
OMELETTE (the food with added worms)
MABEL (the robot housemaid)
KRAFTWERK (the German band who played live)
FISHING (glow-in-the-dark fishing rods featured on the show)
PAPER (the material from which future clothes might be made)
BICYCLE (the floating device predicted to revolutionize future transport)

Page 153: David Attenborough
Hidden Wildlife
1. GORILLA: We'll either get to the safari camp by drivin<u>g, or I'll</u> arrange a helicopter flight.
2. PORCUPINE: Did he say bring a ca<u>p, or cup? I ne</u>ver know what to bring on these expeditions.
3. TORTOISE: Where did you send the camera opera<u>tor to? I se</u>arched high and low but they're not on set.
4. OCTOPUS: It would cause absolute hav<u>oc to pu</u>sh the filming schedule into hurricane season!

What's in a Name?
1. *Zaglossus attenboroughi* – Attenborough's long-beaked echidna
2. *Pristimantis attenboroughi* – Attenborough's rubber frog
3. *Platysaurus attenboroughi* – Attenborough's flat lizard
4. *Electrotettix attenboroughi* – pygmy locust
5. *Attenborosaurus conybeari* – marine reptile
6. *Trigonopterus attenboroughii* – flightless weevil

CHAPTER 8: CHILDREN'S TELEVISION

Page 157: Early Children's TV
Watch with Mother
Monday: *Picture Book*
Tuesday: *Andy Pandy*
Wednesday: *Flower Pot Men*
Thursday: *Rag, Tag and Bobtail*
Friday: *The Woodentops*

Muffin the Mule
1. Kirri the Kiwi
2. Zebbie the Zebra
3. Hubert the Hippopotamus
4. Sally the Seal
5. Grace the Giraffe
6. Oswald the Ostrich
7. Peregrine the Penguin

Page 159: All-Time Favourites
Sound and Vision
1. 'Postman Pat and his black and white cat' (A)
2. 'The Wombles of Wimbledon Common are we' (F)
3. 'There's so much to see, so Come Outside' (D)
4. 'Bill and Ben The Flowerpot Men' (C)
5. 'He's always on the scene: Fireman Sam!' (E)
6. 'What's the story in Balamory, wouldn't you like to know?' (B)

Page 161: *The Magic Roundabout*
Spin the Carousel
Eight; Dylan – the musician was Bob Dylan; Snail;
Magic; Three; Organ

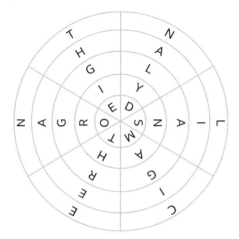

In a Roundabout Way

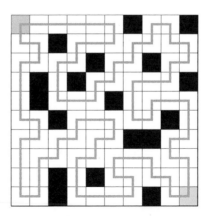

Page 163: *Bagpuss*
Lost and Found

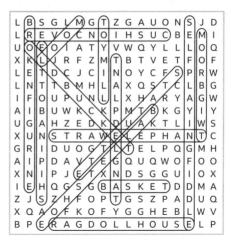

The item not appearing is the LEPRECHAUN – which the characters had first assumed was playing the self-playing fiddle.

Little Mysteries
1. Orange
2. Athens – owls are a symbol of the city of Athens
3. The Archers – after Walter Gabriel
4. Canterbury – at the Beaney House of Art and Knowledge
5. Bertrand Russell

Page 165: *Blue Peter*
Pet Names

The hidden final pet is a dog, Lucy. The other names fit into the grid as follows:

Badge of Honour

The badges and their rules are given below, from left to right, top to bottom, as shown in the puzzle:

1   Blue Badge: Awarded to those who send interesting letters or items for the programme, as well as those who appear on the show
2   Green Badge: Awarded to those who complete pledges to help the environment
3   Silver Badge: Awarded to those who already have a blue badge, and send in an interesting letter or item
4   Purple Badge: Awarded to those who join the Blue Peter fan club
5   Music Badge: Awarded to those who learn a musical instrument or are in a musical performance
6   Sport Badge: Awarded to those who take up a new sport
7   Orange Badge: Awarded to competition winners and runners-up
8   Gold Badge: Awarded in exceptional circumstances, and only to those with an existing badge, for an outstanding achievement such as saving someone's life

Page 167: *Horrible Histories*
Terrific Titles

Awful Egyptians (TEA SPYING)
Gorgeous Georgians (SORE AGING)
Groovy Greeks (KEGERS)
Rotten Romans (NO ARMS)
Slimy Stuarts (STRATUS)
Terrible Tudors (ROT SUD)
Vicious Vikings (SKIVING)
Vile Victorians (SIN TO VICAR)

Famous Figures

From left to right, the following figures are depicted: Edward De Vere; Julius Caesar; Mary Shelley; Charles Dickens; Ernest Shackleton; Ramesses II

Page 169: Classic Animation
Round Them Up

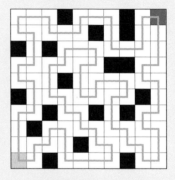

Flower Pot Men

The turtle's name is SLOWCOACH.
Cow; Howl; Owl; Shoal; Sow
Other words to be found include: also, chaos, chow, chows, coal, coals, cowl, cowls, cows, halo, halos, how, howls, loch, lochs, low, lows, owls, scow, scowl, show, who and whoa.

Page 171: *Teletubbies*
Telling Teletubbies Tips

Tinky Winky is purple, has a triangular antenna and has a red bag
Dispy is green, has a straight antenna and has a hat
Laa-Laa is yellow, has a spiral antenna and has an orange ball
Po is red, has a circular antenna and has a blue scooter

The Voice Trumpets

David Walliams
Teresa Gallagher
Fearne Cotton
Rochelle Humes
Jim Broadbent

Page 175: TV Chefs
The Delia Effect

1. CRANBERRIES + K
2. EGGS + I
3. FROZEN AUBERGINE + P
4. LEMON ZESTERS + P
5. OMELETTE PANS + E
6. PRUNES + R
7. SKEWERS + P
8. STOCK CUBES + A
9. SEA SALT + T
10. RHUBARB + E

The revealed dish is KIPPER PATE.

Three-Part Recipe

Ainsley Harriott: *Ready, Steady, Cook*
James Martin: *Junior Bake Off*
Jamie Oliver: *The Naked Chef*
Keith Floyd: *Far Flung Floyd*
Nadiya Hussain: *Nadiya's Fast Flavours*
Nigella Lawson: *Cook, Eat, Repeat*

Page 177: *Saturday Kitchen*
A Good Fit

The surnames are:

Anna CHANCELLOR
Ashley BANJO
Bill BAILEY
Danny MILLER
Dawn FRENCH
Ed GAMBLE
Fearne COTTON
Grace DENT
Gregory PORTER
Helen GLOVER
Jay BLADES
Jessie WARE
Jim DALE
Jo BRAND
Levison WOOD
Mica PARIS
Michael BALL
Naughty BOY
Nick FROST
Paloma FAITH
Sally FIELD
Sara COX
Scott MILLS
Suzi PERRY
Vick HOPE

```
                                  H
            B O Y     W O O D     D
            A                 P       C
          B R A N D     P E R R Y     W
          A     J     P       O       A
          L   C O T T O N   G L O V E R
          L       R           K       E
            F A I T H       A
          G     I       E       N   D E N T
          A     E   F R O S T   A
          M I L L E R         L
          B     D   E   B A I L E Y     P
          L     N   L               A
          E       C H A N C E L L O R
                  H     D   O           I
                        E   X           S
            M I L L S
```

Page 179: *Masterchef*
Winning Menus

The winners and their menus are as follows, with starter, main and dessert listed in that order, plus finally the method of encryption:

Jane Devonshire (an evonshir)
Seafood toast (eafoo oas)
Braised lamb shoulder (raise am houlde)
Rhubarb and custard (hubar n ustar)
First and last letters of each word removed

Thomas Frake (Ekarf Samoht)
Monkfish scampi (Ipmacs hsifknom)
Braised ox cheek (Keehc xo desiarb)
Salted caramel custard tart (Trat dratsuc)
Each entry written backwards

Saliha Mahmood-Ahmed (Slh Mhmd-hmd)
Venison kebab (Vnsn kbb)
Kashmiri duck (Kshmr dck)
Panna cotta (Pnn ctt)
All vowels removed

Sporting Chefs

Reading along the row:
Matt Dawson + Salmon Carpaccio
Greg Rutherford + Scotch Egg
Phil Vickery + Lamb Fillet
Kadeena Cox + Tempura Prawn

Page 181: Gardening Shows
Flower Fit

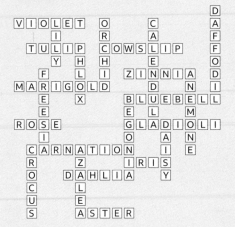

Flower Find

The flower is NASTURTIUM.

1. Always grow MINT in pots – it grows fast and might take over the garden.
2. Leek RUST can also be a problem for garlic, onions and chives.
3. Use a trellis to TRAIN clematis up and along a wall.
4. AUTUMN is the best time to plant garlic.
5. House MARTINS are insectivores and great organic pest controllers.

Page 183: *Changing Rooms*
Interlocking Rooms

1. ATTIC and PORCH
2. CELLAR and LOUNGE
3. OFFICE and PANTRY
4. NURSERY and LIBRARY
5. KITCHEN and BEDROOM
6. BATHROOM and LAVATORY

Piece It Together

In the order given on the page, the clues can be solved as follows:

- DIY
- LLB
- PVC
- MDF
- BBC
- PVA

These can be placed into the grid so as to reveal the word CYMBAL:

CHAPTER 10: NEWS, WEATHER AND CURRENT AFFAIRS

Page 187: News History
News News News

1. LIQUID News
2. News AFTER NOON
3. NewsBEAT
4. NewsCAST
5. NewsNIGHT
6. NewsROOM
7. NewsROUND
8. NewsWATCH
9. YOUR News

When the News Was New

'Rowdy' meeting involving Winston Churchill; Train robbery; Reported sale of a rare Shakespearean folio; Billiards scores; Weather forecast

Page 189: The *Today* Programme
Sue-doku

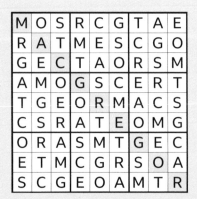

The word spelled is MACGREGOR, referring to Sue MacGregor – whose first name is clued in the puzzle title, 'Sue-doku'.

The Schedule for Today

Newspaper headlines; weather forecast; business news; CEO interview; Political discussion; Thought for the Day

Page 191: Political Interviews
Order of the Days

- National Health Service is established (1948)
- UK joins the European Economic Community (1973)
- Falklands War begins (1982)
- Margaret Thatcher resigns (1990)
- Tony Blair's 'New Labour' wins a landslide general election (1997)
- David Cameron forms a coalition government (2010)
- Scottish independence referendum returns a 'no' vote (2014)
- UK votes to leave the EU (2016)

The date of the first *Newsnight* broadcast was 30/01/1980.

Dodge the Question

Page 193: Satire
Have I Got Presenters for You

1. Kirsty Young (*Desert Island Discs*)
2. Gary Lineker (*Match of the Day*)
3. Dara Ó Briain (*Mock the Week*)
4. Victoria Coren Mitchell (*Only Connect*)
5. Alexander Armstrong (*Pointless*)
6. David Dimbleby (*Question Time*)
7. Jo Brand (*The Great British Bake Off: An Extra Slice*)
8. Anne Robinson (*The Weakest Link*)
9. Jeremy Clarkson (*Top Gear*)

A. Alexander Armstrong
B. Jeremy Clarkson
C. Boris Johnson

Lord Privy Seal

1. Home Secretary
2. Black Rod
3. Chief Whip
4. Speaker

Page 195: *Election Night*
Order, Order

- Sir Alec Douglas-Home, who was in office for 363 days, is excluded.
- Harold WILSON appears twice on the list. He served both before and after Edward Heath.

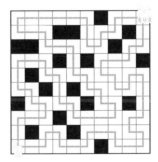

Swingometer Swings

The words and their shifts are as follows:

1. EXIT POLL (+3)
2. PORTILLO MOMENT (–4)
3. SEAT (+5)
4. MAJORITY (–2)
5. HUNG PARLIAMENT (+1)
6. ELECTION (–1)
7. CAMPAIGN (–3)
8. MANIFESTO (+2)

Page 197: Royal Events
The Carriage Ride

Wedding Bells
A. Prince Harry and Meghan Markle
B. Prince Charles and Diana Spencer
C. Prince William and Catherine Middleton
D. Princess Anne and Mark Phillips

Page 199: BBC Weather
Whatever the Weather
- WIND
- RAIN
- HAIL
- BLIZZARD
- THUNDER
- SUNSHINE
- FOG
- LIGHTNING
- DRIZZLE
- GUSTS
- SLEET
- CLOUD
- BREEZE

1. b. North Yorkshire, where the word 'BLIZZARD' is spelled out
2. THUNDER and LIGHTNING
3. Aberdeen: the east coast has SUNSHINE forecast, while the west coast shows FOG
4. HAIL

Page 201: *Shipping Forecast*
Sea Areas
A. Viking
B. North Utsire
C. South Utsire
D. Forties
E. Cromarty
F. Forth
G. Tyne
H. Dogger
I. Fisher
J. German Bight
K. Humber
L. Thames
M. Dover
N. Wight
O. Portland
P. Plymouth
Q. Biscay
R. Trafalgar
S. FitzRoy
T. Sole
U. Lundy
V. Fastnet
W. Irish Sea
X. Shannon
Y. Rockall
Z. Malin
AA. Hebrides
BB. Bailey
CC. Fair Isle
DD. Faeroes
EE. Southeast Iceland

Shipping Forecast Trivia
1. Sailing By
2. FitzRoy
3. 380 words, for the 0048 broadcast, or 350 words for the other broadcasts
4. Coastal weather stations

Page 203: Regional and National News
Lost in the Airwaves

1.	Bristol	BBC Points West
2.	Manchester	BBC North West Tonight
3.	Birmingham	BBC Midlands Today
4.	Leeds	BBC Look North (Leeds)
5.	Cambridge	BBC Look East
6.	Nottingham	BBC East Midlands Today
7.	Plymouth	BBC Spotlight
8.	London	BBC London News
9.	St Helier	BBC Channel Islands
10.	Royal Tunbridge Wells	BBC South East Today
11.	Southampton	BBC South Today

Home Sweet Home
BBC PACIFIC QUAY
The additional words are bay, cab, cap, icy, pay, yap and qua.

Page 205: World Service
List in Translation
The outlines, languages and their native-language equivalents are shown here:

Poland
Polish
Polski

Croatia
Croatian
Hrvatski

Czechia
Czech
Čeština

Hungary
Hungarian
Magyar

Netherlands
Dutch
Nederlands

Finland
Finnish
Suomi

France
French
Français

Italy
Italian
Italiano

CHAPTER 11: TECHNOLOGY

Page 209: Digital
Lost in the Web
The sections visited are, in order:
- News
- Sport
- Weather
- iPlayer
- Sounds
- CBBC
- CBeebies
- Food
- Bitesize
- Local
- Taster

P	L	A	Y	S	O	L	O
I	R	E	E	R	U	E	C
A	T	H	S	D	N	Z	A
E	B	B	C	E	S	I	L
W	C	C	B	T	I	A	T
T	P	S	E	D	B	S	T
R	O	S	E	O	O	F	E
N	E	W	B	I	E	S	R

Section Selection
1. 'Check out this incredible rainbow fish!' – CBBC
2. 'F1 releases new overtaking guidelines' – BBC Sport
3. 'Pack Mr Bumble's spotty bag' – CBeebies
4. 'Should extinct species be brought back to life?' – BBC Bitesize
5. 'Slow cooker hacks to save you money and effort' – BBC Food
6. 'Strange UFO clouds spotted over Cumbria' – BBC Weather

Page 211: Computing
BASIC word puzzle

Page 213: Interactive
True or False?
1. TRUE (T) – but the press release was an April Fools' joke
2. FALSE (O) – it only goes up to 11
3. TRUE (P)
4. TRUE (G)
5. FALSE (E) – the codename was 'Project Barcelona'
6. FALSE (A) – viewers need a TV licence to access iPlayer content, whether live or on catch-up
7. TRUE (R)

The most-watched programme on iPlayer in 2009 was TOP GEAR.

Pick a Number
1. 101
2. 888
3. 555
4. 100
5. 300

PICTURE CREDITS